VICTORIA

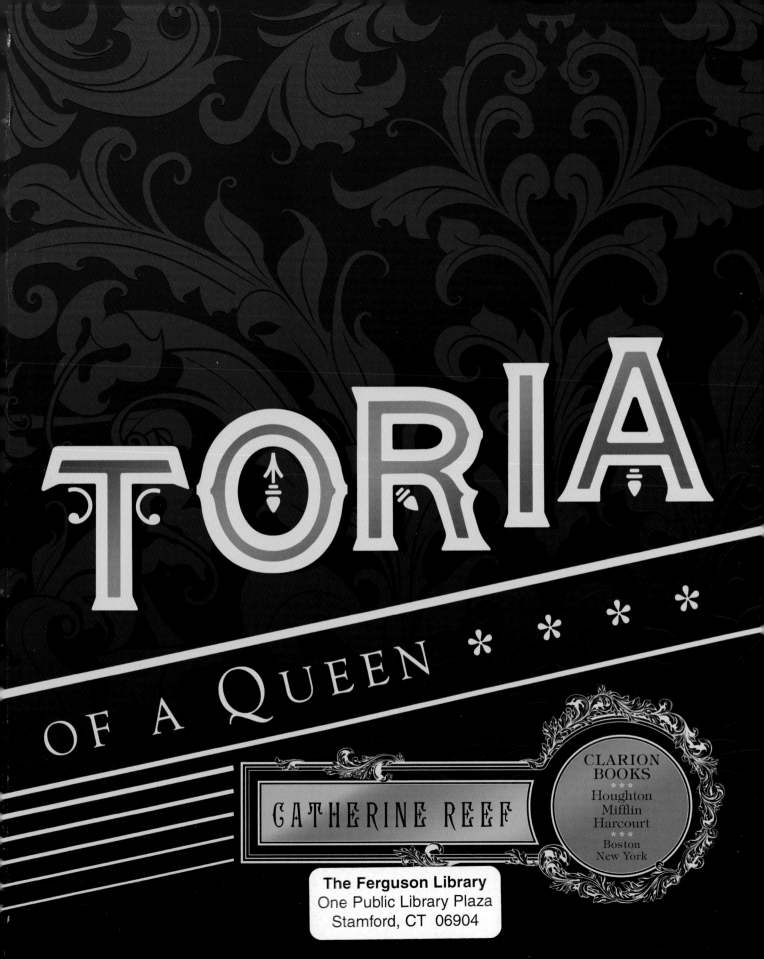

TORIA

OF A QUEEN * * * * *

CATHERINE REEF

CLARION
BOOKS
* * *
Houghton
Mifflin
Harcourt
* * *
Boston
New York

CLARION BOOKS

3 Park Avenue, 19th Floor, New York, New York 10016

Clarion Books is an imprint of Houghton Mifflin Harcourt Publishing Company.

WWW.HMHCO.COM

The text was set in ITC Tiffany Std.
Frames and decorative elements © by Shutterstock
Book design by Sharismar Rodriguez

LIBRARY OF CONGRESS CATALOGING-IN-PUBLICATION DATA

Names: Reef, Catherine, author. * Title: Victoria : portrait of a queen / Catherine Reef.
Description: Boston : Clarion Books ; Houghton Mifflin Harcourt, [2017] * Includes
bibliographical references and index. * Audience: Ages 12 and up. * Identifiers: LCCN
2016050621 | ISBN 9780544716148 (hardcover) * Subjects: LCSH: Victoria, Queen
of Great Britain, 1819-1901—Juvenile literature. * Classification: LCC DA557 .R44 2017
DDC 941.081092 [B]—dc23 * LC record available at https://lccn.loc.gov/2016050621

MANUFACTURED IN CHINA | SCP 10 9 8 7 6 5 4 3 2 1 | 4500665321

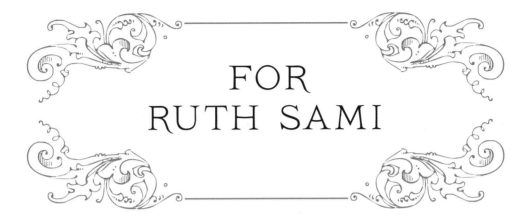

FOR
RUTH SAMI

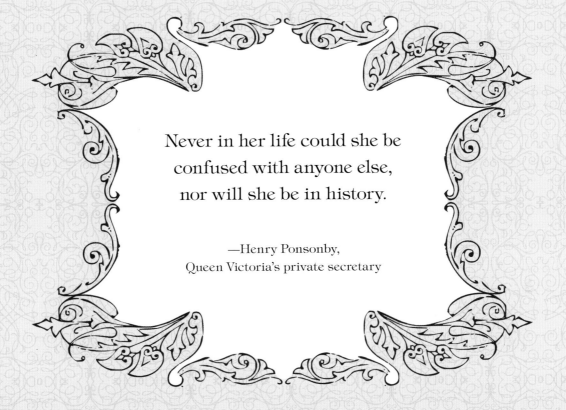

Never in her life could she be
confused with anyone else,
nor will she be in history.

—Henry Ponsonby,
Queen Victoria's private secretary

CONTENTS

LONG LIVE THE QUEEN!

GAWKERS FILLED LONDON'S streets, blocking traffic. It was impossible to get a horse-drawn cab "for love or money," griped one highborn lady. People shoved; carriage drivers grew cross and shouted. "The uproar, the confusion, the crowd, the noise, are indescribable," a man wrote in his diary. The city was "all mob, thronging, bustling, gaping, and gazing at everything, at anything, or at nothing." It was June 28, 1838. Four hundred thousand people had poured into London to celebrate the crowning of Queen Victoria.

The young queen herself had gone to bed the night before with a sense of foreboding, "a feeling that something awful was going to happen." Cannons firing a salute yanked her from sleep at four that morning. A few

hours later, after nibbling at breakfast, she stepped out under a clearing sky and into a coach pulled by horses the color of clotted cream. She hoped no one would notice her fatigue or nerves.

At ten o'clock, trumpets blared and eyes turned toward the palace. The state procession was getting under way. Foreign ambassadors rode first, followed by government ministers and the sprawling royal family. The next twelve coaches carried the queen's attendants and behind them marched soldiers and military officers. Bands played and the crowd hurrahed, despite being held back by armed policemen. Then the spectators caught sight of the queen.

They saw a tiny girl just nineteen years old. She wore a robe of white satin and red velvet. She had large blue eyes and a circlet of diamonds atop her brown hair. Victoria bowed to the left and right. She smiled at admirers waving their

The coronation procession departs for Westminster Abbey. Queen Victoria rides in the company of a lady in waiting.

handkerchiefs and hats. The coronation was to be both solemn and showy, an age-old ritual and a gala affair. Victoria had ascended to the throne on June 20, 1837, upon the death of her uncle King William IV. Her coronation, a formality, had taken a year to plan.

The throng let out a roar when Victoria reached Westminster Abbey, the historic church where, since 1066, the nation's kings and queens had been crowned. More cheers erupted as she stepped inside: "God save Queen Victoria! Long live Queen Victoria! May the Queen live for ever!"

No queen lives forever, but Victoria was to reign for a very long time: sixty-three years, seven months, and two days. Victoria was Britain's longest-reigning monarch until September 9, 2015, when Queen Elizabeth II broke her record. Her subjects knew her as a girl on the cusp of womanhood, then as a busy working mother, and

Queen Victoria (left) enjoys a cup of cocoa while traveling by train in this nineteenth-century advertisement.

too soon as a heartbroken widow. In time, images of the mature queen—short and round, wearing a lacy veil and tiny crown—were everywhere. They graced magazines, postage stamps, and packages of soap and tea.

The years Victoria sat on the throne, from 1837 until 1901, are remembered as the Victorian age. It was a period of great change, when steam power and factories turned agricultural Britain into the industrial leader of the world. One after another, railroads crisscrossed the land, linking cities and villages. Most people traveled overland by coach or on horseback when Victoria became queen; by the 1890s, twenty-nine trains left for London from the northwestern city of Manchester every day. Industrialization shook up society, bringing wealth and status to many people and poverty and dislocation to many others. Prosperous families in houses packed with heavy furniture form one picture of Victorian life. Ragged mothers and children huddled in London doorways make up another.

During the Victorian era, British authors gave the world such unforgettable characters as Sherlock Holmes, Ebenezer Scrooge, Black Beauty, and Alice, the girl who went down a rabbit hole. Scientific progress forced people to question their beliefs. If the great diversity of life on earth had evolved through natural selection as Charles Darwin proposed in 1859, even religious faith had to be reexamined.

Queen Victoria stood for continuity in this shifting, uncertain time. She was an example of strength and patriotism when the nation went to war. Her support of Britain's fighting men endeared her to many. She championed British progress in technology. She was also the subject of scandal.

Victoria reigned over an empire that spanned the globe. The British claimed possessions in the Americas, Africa, India, Asia, Australia, and New Zealand. For good reason people said of Great Britain, "On her dominions the sun never sets." The colonies enriched the mother country. They provided raw materials for British factories, tea for porcelain teacups, and sugar to sweeten it.

The days when kings and queens waged their own wars, made their own laws, and ordered beheadings were long gone when Victoria was crowned. She enjoyed

Passengers crowd London's Paddington Station.
People learned to rely on the speed and convenience
of rail travel during Queen Victoria's reign.

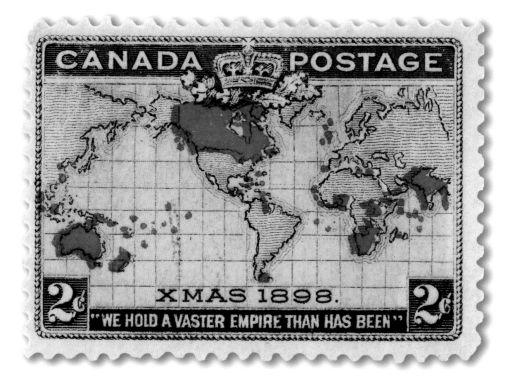

In 1898, Canada issued a postage stamp showing the British Empire spanning the globe. Beginning in 1867, the Dominion of Canada became a self-governing nation but remained part of the empire. Today Canada belongs to the Commonwealth of Nations, an organization of fifty-three independent states, most of which once made up the British Empire.

limited power. She could advise the members of Parliament, but they made laws and set policy. It was her role to be above party politics, to be fair and considerate in her dealings with others.

Victoria tried to be the queen her nation expected, but it was hard for her to live in the public eye. She had trouble controlling her fiery emotions. Time and again she erupted in reckless anger or gave way to torrents of tears. There were days when she exasperated everyone: her family, government leaders, and the British people. She never did anything halfway. When she fell in love, she did so with her

whole heart and soul. When she grieved, it was as though sorrow flowed through her body instead of blood.

Yet she also had great stamina. Even when she felt sad enough to swear that she could not go on, she always did. She was rarely ill and gave birth to many children with little difficulty, at a time when childbirth was painful and dangerous. Many women died after having babies, often from infection. She could accomplish a great deal of work and withstand the mental strain of crises at home and abroad. "The vein of iron that runs thro' her most extraordinary character enables her to bear up to the last minute, like nobody else," said Lady Sarah Lyttelton, her children's nurse.

"People were taken by surprise by the sheer force of her personality," observed Bishop Randall Davidson, who served in the chapel at Windsor Castle during Victoria's reign. "It may seem strange, but it is true that as a woman she was both shy and humble. . . . But as Queen she was neither shy nor humble and asserted her position unhesitatingly."

Despite her premonition from the night before, nothing awful happened on her coronation day. Life, with all its joys and hard lessons, stretched before Victoria like a long, rolling palace lawn. And when the festivities were over, she went home and gave her little spaniel, Dash, his bath.

CHAPTER I

ENGLAND'S HOPE

IF ANOTHER PRINCESS had not died tragically and young, Victoria never would have been born.

The ill-fated princess was Charlotte. She was the only child of the prince regent, the man who occupied the British throne. The prince was ruling in place of his father, King George III, who had been deemed mentally ill. Upon his father's death, the prince regent would be crowned King George IV. Charlotte was twenty-one years old on November 6, 1817, when she delivered a stillborn son. Within hours she sickened, and soon Charlotte too was dead.

The English people had loved the princess. "She stood on high," wrote a newspaperman. Charlotte had embodied "images of youth, and promise, and blooming womanhood." Eighteen months before, the public had rejoiced in Charlotte's marriage to handsome Prince Leopold of Saxe-Coburg. They had felt secure knowing that she would reign one day, upon her father's death, all in good time.

Now there would be no Queen Charlotte, and England mourned. Her loss was "a sad and dire accident calculated to fill with tears the eyes of almost all," noted

In 1817 the British people mourned the death of Princess Charlotte, who stood for virtue and goodness amid a corrupt royal family.

one English writer. Charlotte had been the lone beacon of virtue in a royal family clouded by vice. Everyone knew that her father, the prince regent, had a mistress. He ran up huge debts, which the government paid with taxes collected from the people.

The prince regent had a string of younger brothers who stood in line to inherit the throne, but none of them had an heir to carry on the royal line after him. Closest in age to the prince regent was Prince Frederick, the Duke of York. He was separated from his wife and, like his brothers, had a mistress. Next came Prince William, the Duke of Clarence. He lived openly and quite merrily with his mistress and their ten children— none of them legitimate, and all forbidden by law to be king or queen. Fourth in line to the throne was forty-nine-year-old Prince Edward, the Duke of Kent. He was a former army officer who had been living for decades with his French mistress, whom he loved. In a society that scorned unmarried couples living together and single women bearing children, the princes brazenly broke the rules.

Now, with Charlotte dead, a race was on. Which of these royal rogues would be the first to father a legitimate child and heir? The Duke of York was out of the running from the start. Even if he returned to his wife, she was too old to bear children. The Duke of Clarence wasted no time and threw his mistress and large brood out of the house. He proposed to one rich young woman after another until

at last one accepted him. She was a German princess half his age, Adelaide of Saxe-Meiningen.

The ex-army man, Edward, Duke of Kent, said goodbye forever to his adored mistress, who in all their years together had never borne a child. "My brothers are not so strong as I am; I have lived a regular life. I shall outlive them all," he told himself. "The crown will come to me and my children."

Edward carried too much weight on his frame. He had bulging eyes and dyed whiskers, and his breath reeked of garlic. But his military bearing and fine manners

ALL the WORLD'S a STAGE. —— And one man in his time plays many parts &c &c

King George IV, formely the prince regent, rests a gouty foot as he sits before portraits of himself at different stages in life. The cartoonist implies that George pursued amusement and neglected his health.

made him attractive in some women's eyes. He stood tall and straight in his red army coat and walked with an officer's confidence. In company he was modest and sure of himself. He never yawned or whistled or put his legs up on chairs. At dinner he offered the best dishes to others.

His search for a bride took him to Germany, where he wooed a princess named Victoire. She happened to be the sister of Prince Leopold, husband of the late Princess Charlotte. A widow living in a secluded castle, Victoire was thirty-one years old and spoke no English. If she was not a beauty, at least she had a pleasant smile. Her hair and eyes were brown, and her body was solid and shapely. Victoire had two children, Karl and Feodora, ages thirteen and ten. They were proof that she was fertile.

The couple married, and soon Victoire was pregnant. Edward wanted the baby born in England, so that no one there would ever question the child's birth date or parentage. On March 28, 1819, with winter nearly over and Victoire starting her eighth month of pregnancy, the pair transported their household across the English Channel. They settled into rooms at London's Kensington Palace, which had housed British royalty since 1689. On May 24, in a lushly carpeted bedchamber festooned with draperies, the Duchess of Kent gave birth to a daughter.

The little girl was "as plump as a partridge," her ecstatic father boasted. She was perfection, "a model of strength and beauty combined." He hovered over visitors, telling them, "Look at her well, for she will be Queen of England." The wee girl was fifth in line to the throne, preceded by three uncles—the prince regent and the dukes of York and Clarence—and her father. Because Tsar Alexander of Russia had asked to be a godfather to her, she was christened Alexandrina. Victoria, her second name, honored her mother. She soon became known as Princess Victoria.

The Duke of Kent had never learned to be thrifty. He filled his family's living quarters with gilded mirrors and ornate furniture. When he turned fifty-two, on November 2, he threw himself a lavish party. Then, having spent far beyond his

Kensington Palace as it looked in 1819, the year Princess Victoria was born.

means, he asked the prince regent for money. The ruler ignored the request, being short of cash himself.

Hoping to live more cheaply outside London, the duke and duchess moved their family to a cottage beside Lyme Bay, on England's southern coast. They dreamed of sea bathing and salty air, but they arrived on Christmas Day, with wind howling and snow falling. In no time at all, the duke came down with a cold. His cough worsened and his fever soared as the cold turned into pneumonia. Doctors removed six pints of his blood, employing a standard medical practice later proven to be useless and even dangerous. When he showed no improvement, they bled him again.

Weak and struggling to breathe, the duke drew up a will making Victoire the sole guardian of their daughter and leaving what little property he had to his wife. On Sunday morning, January 23, having put his affairs in order, the duke died. His

death left Princess Victoria fourth in line to the throne. When King George III died six days later and the prince regent was crowned King George IV, Victoria moved up the line to spot number three.

What was Victoire to do? Not only was she a widowed mother with no money, but she was stranded in a country where she barely spoke the language. She felt thankful for the nearness of her brother, Prince Leopold. He appealed to the royal family and gained permission for Victoire to occupy her husband's old apartment in Kensington Palace. Leopold also gave his sister a yearly allowance of two thousand pounds, which he raised to three thousand within a short time. Parliament granted the duchess an annual income of six thousand pounds in 1825, to provide for the princess, and another ten thousand per year in 1831. Still, the duchess complained that she never had enough. Victoire was a German princess, at least the equal, in her mind, of the wealthier British royals who surrounded her. She felt that she too deserved every regal comfort.

In this way, Kensington Palace became Princess Victoria's home. As a baby she crawled on its yellow carpets. As a child she rode a donkey through its acres of gardens. She tiptoed up the Great Staircase to study murals crowded with portraits of courtiers from times gone by. Little Victoria watched important personages come and go—lords and ladies, princes and dukes. Her face brightened if she saw her stout uncle Frederick, the Duke of York, who gave her presents and threw her a party with a Punch and Judy show. But she hid her eyes if she spotted a bishop in a frightening wig.

Victoria could be a stubborn, defiant child who flashed her blue eyes and threw tantrums to get her way. There were storms of tears when she had to wash up in the morning, and more storms when it was time to get dressed. She once flung a pair of scissors at Fraulein Louise Lehzen, her German-born governess. "She drives me at times into real desperation," complained her exasperated mother.

The princess howled and stamped her foot if her tutor, the Reverend George Davys, told her to sit still for a reading lesson. When he asked her to make an

As a child Victoria played on the Great Staircase at Kensington Palace.

"h" with her pencil, she insisted on making an "o." The next day, Davys noted in his diary, "When we were to begin our copy of 'o's,' Princess Victoria wished for 'h's.'" Not daring to criticize royalty, he remarked, "She seems to be a sweet-tempered child." The princess was much happier when Davys turned schoolwork into a game. She liked it when he wrote simple words on cards, placed them around the room, and asked her to fetch them. Soon he could write in his diary, "The little Princess has made very considerable progress in her reading." Victoria learned to

solve arithmetic problems and to speak French, German, and a little Italian. She memorized names and dates from Europe's history and pointed out the countries of the world on maps.

Masters came to Kensington Palace to instruct her in drawing, music, and dance. She showed talent as an artist, sang in a pleasing soprano voice, and danced prettily. She detested practicing the piano, though. When the music master told her that she must, she slammed shut the lid on the keyboard. "There! You see there is no *must* about it," she declared.

Years later, Victoria recalled her childhood as lonely. She slept every night in her mother's room and played with her half sister, Feodora. But Feodora was twelve years older than Victoria, and in 1828 she married a German prince and went off to live in his castle. Nine-year-old Victoria turned to her painted wooden dolls, but she longed for real children her own age.

Victoria's mother felt lonely too. The Duchess of Kent never mastered English, and her daughter's royal relatives disliked her. Her brother Leopold went away in June 1831, leaving her "friendless and alone," she said. The newly independent nation of Belgium had asked Leopold to be its king, and he had accepted. At least there was one person to offer guidance and speak soothing words: her late husband's personal assistant, a schemer named John Conroy.

Conroy was a handsome dark-haired man who knew how to flatter and please. The son of Irish parents, he had begun his working life a soldier. Eager to move up in the world, he married a general's daughter. In 1817, he entered the duke's service. After the duke died, he did whatever it took to secure a place that offered him money and influence. He gained the confidence of the king's unmarried sister, Princess Sophia, and soon had control of her purse. He talked Princess Sophia into persuading the king to dub him a knight and make the governess, Fraulein Lehzen, a baroness.

He also offered his services to Victoire, Duchess of Kent. The duchess possessed

little wealth for Conroy to get his hands on, but she had a child who would likely reign over England one day. Conroy saw that gaining favor with mother and daughter today might let him wield power tomorrow.

He convinced the duchess that Victoria was never to be alone. If she left a room, a servant had to go with her; if she went downstairs, someone had to hold her hand. She was not to speak to any visitor unless a third person was present, and she was to be kept apart from the rest of the royal family. He whispered in the duchess's ear that without these measures Victoria could be poisoned, but his true purpose was to tighten his hold. He reminded the duchess that the little princess was the "Nation's Hope." The constant surveillance made childhood a sad, anxious time for Princess Victoria. She grew to detest Sir John Conroy, and she hated his daughter Victoire, whom he thrust on her as a playmate.

Conroy's placid, amiable wife admired her husband and believed he was on his way up in the world. But people in England's palaces were talking and assuming the worst. They asked one another what kind of relationship the Duchess of Kent enjoyed with John Conroy, a married man with six children. Victoria's aunt Adelaide, the German princess who married Prince William, the Duke of Clarence, cautioned Victoria's mother. The Conroys were "not of so high a rank that they *alone* should be the entourage and the companions of the future Queen of England," she said. The Duchess of Kent acted as though she had not heard a word.

With passing years, it seemed more likely that Victoria would indeed be England's queen. When her favorite uncle, the Duke of York, died in 1827, she became the second person in line to the throne, behind her uncle the Duke of Clarence. Then, on June 26, 1830, King George IV died of a ruptured blood vessel in his stomach. The Duke of Clarence was crowned King William IV. His wife would now be known as Queen Adelaide, and the person who would rule Britain if William should die was his eleven-year-old niece.

Victoire, Duchess of Kent, and little Victoria.

The conniving John Conroy was after money and power.

The nation would never permit a child to act as head of state. If William were to die before Victoria reached eighteen, the age of majority, Parliament would appoint a regent to conduct official business in her place, as George IV, then prince regent, had done on behalf of his father. The Duchess of Kent wanted the regency for herself should such a situation arise, and John Conroy wanted it for her too.

The duchess and Conroy feared that the current king and queen might take Victoria away to bring her up in their quarters, surrounded by their attendants, and groom her for her future role. Hoping to prevent this from happening, they kept her out of the king's sight as much as possible. The duchess even refused to let Victoria attend William's coronation, which added to the girl's sadness. Desperate to hang on to their one chance for gaining power, they took the princess on a series of tours to different parts of England. Their purpose was to make Victoria popular with the citizenry and show people that she needed her mother's constant care. Their plan to keep her dependent on them as she grew up had a name: they called it the "Kensington system."

Victoria, the duchess, Conroy, his daughter Victoire, and their servants took their first trip in the summer and fall of 1830. They meandered in central England, stopping in places like Stratford-on-Avon, the famed birthplace of William Shakespeare, and the scenic Malvern Hills, with slopes that shone golden in the

sun. In place after place, people turned out to see the princess, and officials treated her like a grown-up royal visitor. She formally opened a park in the city of Bath, and she toured a porcelain factory in Worcester.

In 1832 the troupe ventured into Wales. Bands and church choirs entertained them, and town leaders gave speeches of welcome. As their beribboned carriage passed through coal-mining districts, Victoria looked out on hardship, which was new to her eyes. "The men, women, children, country and houses are all black," she wrote in her journal, describing the dismal effects of coal dust. "Every where, smoking and burning coal heaps, intermingled with wretched huts and carts and little ragged children."

The third tour began in summer 1833, when Victoria was fourteen. This time the princess brought Dash, whom she dressed up in doll clothes. The travelers visited towns on England's southern shore and boated to the Isle of Wight, four miles off the coast. Victoria and her mother stayed in Norris Castle, which had been built for a wealthy lord in 1799. Most castles were older and had fortifications to keep out enemies, but Norris Castle was strictly for show. Victoria and the duchess strolled in its tidy gardens and savored its scenic views.

As reports of naval ships firing volleys to salute Victoria reached King William's ears, he grew annoyed. William loved being king; he had rarely stopped smiling from the moment he first donned his royal robes. He was fond of his niece, but he hated to think that she might be more popular with his subjects than he was. So he ordered an end to the military salutes in her honor. Henceforward, he decreed, the armed forces were only to salute the king and queen.

When the Duchess of Kent and John Conroy planned another trip in 1835, Victoria protested. Knowing the king disapproved, she asked if they could please stay home. Her mother only scolded. "Can you be dead to the calls your position demands?" she asked. "Turn your thoughts and views to your future station, its duties, and the claims that exist on you." The group departed the next morning.

German-born Louise Lehzen became the princess's governess and trusted friend.

Victoria found nothing to enjoy about this trip. She had been bullied into going, and for much of the time she was sick. Her throat was sore, she had no appetite, and she had trouble falling asleep at night. And it seemed that every time she turned around, John Conroy was waving a piece of paper in her face, trying to make her sign it. He and the duchess wanted her to appoint him as her private secretary. Knowing that her governess—her "beloved Lehzen"—was on her side, Victoria summoned her old stubbornness. "I resisted in spite of my illness," she said. Baroness Lehzen had taught her to hold fast to her principles.

Lehzen was strict with the princess and hardly ever laughed. She had a pointy nose and chin and often complained of headaches. But she was devoted to Victoria and had earned the girl's loyalty and love.

The princess recovered, and in May she turned seventeen. The same month she had a visit from two German cousins, Prince Ernst and Prince Albert. They were the sons of her mother's brother, the Duke of Saxe-Coburg and Gotha. Prince Ernst was a year older than Victoria, but Prince Albert was just her age. He had a serious nature and was pudgy with baby fat, but Victoria thought his face was "full of goodness and sweetness, and very clever and intelligent." Albert felt shy around girls and said only that his cousin was "very amiable." The three teens sat together on a sofa and looked at drawings. The boys played for the princess on the piano. "The more I see them the more I am delighted with them, and the more I love them,"

Victoria wrote in her journal. All too soon Ernst and Albert went home to Germany. "I cried bitterly, very bitterly," Victoria confessed. How hard it was, after these few happy days with young friends, to resume her lonely life.

Princes Ernst and Albert as youths. A lonely Princess Victoria welcomed their friendship.

That summer an invitation came from the king. William was asking the Duchess of Kent and the princess to attend the queen's birthday party on August 13, at Windsor Castle. The king expected his guests to remain at Windsor to celebrate his own birthday eight days later, on August 21. Windsor Castle, for centuries a home to British royalty, was an enormous residence in the county of Berkshire. It contained hundreds of rooms and was the burial site of ten monarchs, including King Henry VIII, whose ghost was rumored to walk its halls.

The duchess replied that she and her daughter would have to miss Queen Adelaide's birthday because they would be in the country celebrating her own, on August 17. She promised, though, to have Victoria at Windsor for the king's party. William was furious. For the duchess to turn down a royal invitation was the height of rudeness. Placing more importance on her own birthday than on the queen's showed disrespect. He grew even angrier when he learned that the duchess had moved herself and Victoria into better rooms at Kensington Palace without asking his permission. She had taken "a most unwarrantable liberty," he said. Who did this woman think she was?

Princess Victoria and her mother arrived at Windsor in time for the king's birthday. At dinner, as the Duchess of Kent sat at his side, the king stood to address the

William IV, an ill man, spent a mere seven years as king. He hoped to live beyond Victoria's
eighteenth birthday so she would reign without interference from her mother or John Conroy.

hundred guests who had gathered. "I trust in God that my life may be spared for nine months longer," he stated, "after which period, in the event of my death, no regency would take place. I should then have the satisfaction of leaving the royal authority to the personal exercise of that young lady"—and he gestured toward Victoria—"and not in the hands of a person now near me, who is surrounded by evil advisers."

The king went on to list his grievances against the Duchess of Kent. Soon he was shouting, and his face grew red. He closed with these words: "For the future I shall insist and command that the Princess do upon all occasions appear at my Court, as it is her duty to do." When the tirade ended, Victoria was in tears. Her mother sat still as a statue. Among the speechless onlookers was an old military hero, the Duke of Wellington. He called the whole scene "very awkward, by God!"

REGINAMANIA

"THAT MY LIFE may be spared nine months longer . . ." It was the wish of a dying man.

King William was seventy-one and in failing health. He had asthma and a weak heart. Climbing stairs left him exhausted and out of breath. He suffered from gout—fiery pain in his joints that made him quick to lose his temper. There were other, more mysterious things wrong with him too. For instance, his neck swelled up from time to time. Would the king live to see Victoria turn eighteen? Or would he die sooner, so that a regent would be named? John Conroy could focus on little else.

By mid-May, the king had lost his appetite and was having fainting spells. He was "in a very odd state," according to his perplexed doctor. But he had planned a ball to celebrate Victoria's eighteenth birthday, on the twenty-fourth, and when that day dawned he was still alive.

The Duchess of Kent, Sir John Conroy, and Lady Conroy all attended the ball, but Victoria chose to travel separately, in her own carriage. She could make

decisions like that now because she had come of age. The trip was slow, with so many people lining the route to St. James's Palace, the king's residence. They were hoping to see the future queen—or "poor stupid me," as Victoria called herself.

Two large palace rooms glowed with brilliant candlelight. In each an orchestra played as the elite of English society danced in diamonds and gleaming splendor. Victoria danced too, and she joined the guests at a banquet. She was the evening's brightest star, but it was hard for her to have a good time. The king was too ill to greet her, and Conroy's suspicious eyes never left her. That night she wrote in her diary that turning eighteen had made her feel old.

Conroy claimed that Victoria seemed younger than her years. He told anyone who would listen that Victoria was "light & frivolous" and "easily caught by fashion and appearances." In truth, Conroy was desperate. Behind the scenes he was pressuring Victoria to say that she wanted a regent appointed until she turned twenty-one. At the very least, she could make Conroy her secretary.

During this time, Baron Stockmar, a friend and advisor to Victoria's uncle King Leopold, called at Kensington Palace. Right away, he saw what was happening. Conroy, he observed, was continuing "the system of intimidation with the genius of a madman." The duchess was completely in his power, doing all that she was instructed to do. The Duchess of Kent nagged Victoria, saying over and over that the British people adored Conroy and wanted to see him in a high position. She cried and carried on and reminded Victoria of the many sacrifices, real or imagined, that she had made for her daughter's sake. So far Victoria had resisted her mother and Conroy, but Stockmar was not resting easy: "Whether she will hold out, Heaven knows," he wrote, "for they plague her, every hour and every day."

She did not have to hold out for long. At six a.m. on June 20, Victoria was awaked with a kiss. She opened her eyes and saw her mother's face. The Duchess of Kent informed her that the Archbishop of Canterbury, the leader of the Church of England, was waiting to see her. Lord Conyngham, the nobleman who oversaw the

royal household, had come as well. They could be there for only one reason: King William IV was dead.

Victoria slipped into her dressing gown and let her mother hold her hand as she hurried downstairs to meet her callers. Lehzen trotted along behind with smelling salts, in case the dizzying turn of events caused one of the women to faint.

When Victoria walked into the sitting room where her visitors waited, she went alone. She recorded in her diary what happened next: "Lord Conyngham then acquainted me that my poor Uncle,

Christian Friedrich, Baron Stockmar, gave sage advice to Victoria's uncle King Leopold of Belgium. Victoria would learn to rely on his counsel too.

the King, was no more, and had expired at 12 minutes past 2 this morning." Victoria was queen.

"Poor man, he was always very kind to me and he *meant* it well I know," the new queen said of her late uncle. "He was odd, very odd, and singular, but his intentions were often ill-interpreted." It was a historic moment. Victoria's life was forever changed. Immediately she went to work, as duty compelled her to do.

That day she met with her Privy Council. She was the head of state, but real power belonged to the cabinet ministers who made up this body. They were chosen by the prime minister from the two houses of Parliament: the House of Commons and the House of Lords. Voters elected representatives to the House of Commons from their borough or county. In the House of Lords sat peers of the realm—dukes, marquesses, earls, viscounts, and barons—and archbishops and bishops of the Church of England. Parliament passed laws that the monarch

In the early-morning hours of June 20, 1837, the Archbishop of Canterbury and Lord Conyngham address Victoria as queen.

approved after listening to advice from her Privy Council. The prime minister was a powerful person, the leader of the majority party in Parliament. If there was an election and the public voted another party into the majority, there would be a new prime minister and a new government formed.

The men of the Privy Council were used to a crusty, impatient old king. They had no idea what to expect from this youthful queen whom they had hardly ever seen. The men wondered how she would conduct herself. Would she be dazzled or dumbfounded by her new position?

They were pleasantly surprised. "There never was anything like the first impression she produced, or the chorus of praise and admiration which is raised about her manner and behaviour," wrote Charles Greville, the council secretary, who kept a detailed diary. Victoria read a speech prepared for her by the prime minister. She stated, "I place my firm reliance upon the wisdom of Parliament and upon the loyalty and affection of my people." She would also "protect the rights, and promote, to the utmost of my power, the happiness and welfare of all classes of my subjects." Said a councilor named John Wilson Croker, "Her voice which is naturally beautiful, was clear and untroubled."

One by one the ministers came forward to show their loyalty by kissing the queen's hand. Victoria handled this formality "with perfect calmness and self-possession, but at the same time with a graceful modesty and propriety," Greville observed. After the meeting, the Duke of Wellington told Greville that if Victoria "had been his own daughter he could not have desired to see her perform her part better."

Victoria took care of other queenly business on that momentous day. She ordered her bed moved from her mother's chamber into a room of her own. She asked her old governess to remain with her as an attendant and friend. And she turned John Conroy out of her household, although he remained close to her mother. That night she asserted her independence by dining alone, without the Duchess of Kent. "I

Victoria had only been queen for a few hours when she met with her Privy Council for the first time. The artist David Wilkie painted her in a white dress, but she wore black because she was in mourning for the late king.

had to remind her *who* I was," she said. As if to remind herself, she wrote in her diary, "I am *Queen.*"

In July, Victoria left Kensington Palace, which held too many reminders of her painful childhood. She chose Buckingham Palace, three miles away, as her London home. Her mother would have rooms there too, but in a distant part of the building. This palace was named for the first Duke of Buckingham, who built a brick house on the site in 1703. King George III purchased the property in 1761 and started remodeling it, but he never completed the work. George IV enlarged the structure into a palace, but he never lived there either.

Victoria's government advisers wished she would choose a more practical place to live. Buckingham Palace's vast rooms were largely unfurnished, but Victoria

thought they held furniture enough. The rooms were still uncarpeted, but Victoria said that she disliked carpets. There were no windows to air out the kitchen, the servants' workrooms were too small, the plumbing functioned badly, and the fireplaces sent more smoke into the rooms than up the chimneys. But none of this made any difference to a queen who had made up her mind. Two days after moving in, she hosted a sumptuous dinner party in her new home.

When she had a few minutes alone to reflect, Victoria vowed to fulfill her duty to her country. "I am very young and perhaps in many, though not in all things, inexperienced," she admitted, "but I am sure that very few have more real good-will and more real desire to do what is fit and right than I have." Knowing she needed guidance, Victoria turned to the suave, worldly prime minister.

William Lamb, Second Viscount Melbourne, was still handsome at fifty-eight. He was clever at conversation, had a sharp wit, and knew how to charm. He seemed at ease with himself and his surroundings and was ever a skilled politician. Melbourne was alone in life; his wife and two children were dead. Sorrow had caused Melbourne to seal up his feelings—until Victoria opened his heart to life. He adopted a fatherly attitude toward the new queen and was generous to her with his time. He went riding with Victoria, dined with her, and sat with her in the evening. He schooled her in her new role and flattered and pleased her. Victoria, who had grown up without a parent she could trust, quickly learned to rely on Melbourne. "There are not *many* like him in this world of deceit," she said. The two became the dearest of friends, although they were forty years apart in age.

Victoria sought Melbourne's advice about personal problems, such as how to deal with her mother. The Duchess of Kent was bombarding Victoria with requests. She expected to be seated in a place of high importance at banquet tables, higher than was proper for the monarch's mother, almost as if she herself were a queen. Such a breach of protocol would upset other members of the royal family, Victoria knew, and she simply could not allow it. The duchess also wanted John Conroy and his family to be received in the palace like nobility. And although Parliament had

Buckingham Palace, as it looked in 1839. The girl walking with a dog on the far side of the lake may be Queen Victoria.

raised her yearly allowance by eight thousand pounds, she was asking for more money to pay off her debts, which exceeded fifty thousand pounds. She had been living a grander life than she could afford. "I never saw so foolish a woman," Melbourne said. He counseled Victoria to stand firm and not to give in to her mother's unreasonable appeals. At the same time, he cautioned patience. For a queen to sever such a close family tie would be unseemly.

She needed to show no restraint, Melbourne said, toward John Conroy, who had his own outlandish demands. Seeing that his schemes for power and fame might soon fail, Conroy was trying to squeeze all he could from his royal connections. He asked for a yearly pension of three thousand pounds. He also wanted Victoria to make him a duke or an earl, which as queen she had the power to do. With Lord Melbourne nodding in approval, Victoria granted Conroy the pension he sought, but she stopped short of making him a peer of the realm. She bestowed on him the title of baronet, which was a little better than knighthood. These concessions were more than Conroy deserved, but they were worth making, Victoria thought, if they would get him out of her life. Still, it took until 1840 for Conroy to accept that he had nothing more to gain. In that year he moved to Italy.

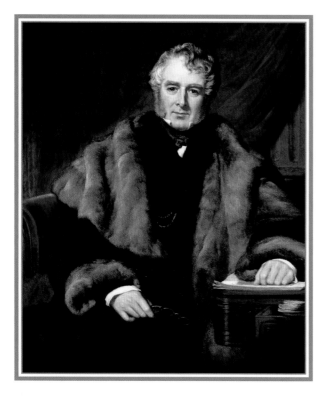

The prime minister, Lord Melbourne, offered his counsel and friendship to the young queen.

Victoria never tired of hearing Lord Melbourne speak. He talked of many things, from Shakespeare's plays to the cannibals dwelling in distant parts of the world. He told her about people from history—some who lived long ago and others he had known, such as her grandfather George III and her uncle George IV. "He knows about everybody and everything; *who* they were and *what* they did," Victoria gushed, "and he imparts all his knowledge in such a *kind* and agreeable manner." He never minded if Dash licked his hand. Victoria and her prime minister laughed with gusto when things amused them, and they indulged in gossip. When Victoria remarked that a Miss Rice, a young lady they knew, was quite tall, Melbourne called her "a great thumping girl"—"which made me laugh very much," Victoria said.

It was so unusual for a prime minister to spend this much time with a reigning monarch that some observers wondered what he was up to. "Take care that Lord Melbourne is not King," the Duchess of Kent warned her daughter. Other people accused Melbourne of influencing the queen to promote his political agenda. "His situation is certainly the most dictatorial, the most despotic, that the world has ever seen," complained Councilor Croker, who was not above stretching the truth.

Melbourne's political party, the Whigs, held progressive views and had support from the rising middle class. The Whigs favored a strong Parliament. They had recently extended the right to vote to more citizens. Before passage of the reform, voting was limited to men who owned property valued at forty shillings or more.

This was a fairly small sum, yet it excluded most men in Britain. The new legislation changed the property requirement so that more men—but not all—were allowed to vote.

Melbourne's critics belonged to the rival party, the Tories, which had many aristocrats as members. The Tories believed in doing things the traditional way and keeping power in the hands of the elite. They looked warily at change. In the early years of Victoria's reign, the Whigs and Tories were starting to be called, respectively, the Liberal and Conservative Parties.

Lord Melbourne had been in government since 1806 and knew better than to mold Victoria's opinions to suit his political goals. The queen was supposed to work willingly with whichever party was in power. Nevertheless, an impressionable young woman was bound to be influenced by a knowledgeable older man. When Melbourne suggested that she appoint wives and female relatives of Whig politicians as her ladies of the bedchamber, for example, she heeded his advice. Like other ladies in waiting, these women held a position of honor, serving as assistants and companions to the queen.

Victoria also received practical advice from her uncle Leopold, who counseled her to weigh decisions carefully. "Whenever a question is of some importance," he instructed, "it should not be decided on the day when it is submitted to you." Leopold said that she must never let people comment on any matter concerning herself unless she has asked for their opinion. If any person dared to make such a remark, she was to "change the conversation, and make the individual feel that he has made a mistake."

Victoria loved her busy days. "It is to me the *greatest pleasure* to do my duty for my country and my people, and no fatigue, however great, will be burdensome to me if it is for the welfare of the nation," she said. Her people were delighted with the new monarch. They snatched up pictures of her as fast as artists could sketch them and printers could produce them. "Of the Queen there have been already above fifty portraits published, good, bad, and indifferent," a magazine

Victoria's uncle Leopold gave her advice gained from his own experience as a reigning monarch.

reported. If Victoria went to the theater or to Windsor, publishers sold pictures of those outings too. Noted one journal, the entire country had come down with "Reginamania." (*Regina* is the Latin word for queen.) "This epidemic continues to prevail to such an extent, that the papers are under the necessity of dwelling constantly upon the beauty not only of the Queen's person and features, but of her *feet,* and even of her *slippers.*"

The new queen had to adjust quickly to the attention. All who met her wanted to look her over and record their impressions. Victoria was "really in person, in face & especially in eyes and complexion, a very nice girl," pronounced Lord Holland, a powerful Whig. "Like the rest of the world I am captivated."

"Her size is below the middle, but her figure is finely proportioned," noted Sallie Coles Stevenson, wife of the American minister in London. Standing not quite four feet, eleven inches, Victoria blamed her shortness on the "worry and torment" of her youth, claiming they had stunted her growth. Stevenson also remarked on Victoria's voice, declaring it "as sweet as a Virginia nightingale's."

Some cranky people were determined to criticize. One was the politician Thomas Creevey, who dined with Victoria one evening. "A more homely little being you never beheld," he said. "She laughs in real earnest, opening her mouth as wide as it can go." He added, "She eats quite as heartily as she laughs, I think I may say she gobbles."

Many nights the queen hosted formal dinners for politicians, diplomats, royal

relatives, and visiting dignitaries. Her rapid eating posed a problem for her guests, especially if they had big appetites. There would be four to six courses, with tasty offerings such as fish with oyster sauce, roast mutton, and meringue tartlets. The queen was served each course first, followed by everyone else, according to their social rank. But once the queen had finished a course, her guests had to stop eating too, and servants cleared the plates away. Those served last barely had a chance to taste their food.

Victoria could easily afford to entertain, since Parliament had voted to give her a yearly allowance of 385,000 pounds, making her one of the world's richest women. She summered at two royal residences, Windsor Castle and Brighton Pavilion, a seaside palace that had been built for George IV. Gleaming white with domes and minarets, the pavilion looked like the Taj Mahal—or like "a collection of stone pumpkins and pepper-boxes," as one observer described it. The late king had filled it with furniture from India and paintings, armor, pottery, and gongs from China. The curios were "so overloaded one upon another, that the effect is more like a china shop," said one guest.

Watchers saw Victoria in all her finery when she carried out her ceremonial duties, such as the opening of Parliament on November 20. This centuries-old tradition marked the annual start of the parliamentary session. For this occasion Victoria wore diamonds in her ears, around her neck, and on her head. She rode in George III's golden coach to the Palace of Westminster, commonly known as the Houses of Parliament. There she walked in a procession to the chamber of the House of Lords, where she sat on a throne. With the Houses of Lords and Commons both in attendance and the galleries packed with spectators, she delivered a short speech laying out legislative goals for the coming year. She urged Parliament to keep spending in check, and she expressed the hope that the lawmakers would soon approve a trade agreement with Bolivia and Peru. She closed by declaring her confidence in their loyalty and wisdom.

CHAPTER III

GROWING PAINS

ON THE QUEEN'S coronation day, June 28, 1838, Westminster Abbey was decked with crimson draperies and flounces, all fringed in gold. Victoria knew that her mother, Lord Melbourne, and her beloved governess, Louise Lehzen, were there, watching her with full hearts. Her half siblings—Victoire's older children, Prince Karl and Princess Feodora—had come all the way from Germany to see her crowned. They joined bejeweled peers and peeresses, foreign dignitaries, and the members of Parliament. Ordinary people lucky enough to get tickets filled a gallery.

The five-hour ceremony took place in a church because it had a religious purpose. Standing before the congregation, Victoria took an oath to uphold not only the laws of the land but also the laws of God. With the Archbishop of Canterbury leading, she and the congregation prayed and sang hymns. The archbishop anointed Victoria with holy oil, because "Kings, Priests, and Prophets" had been so anointed in biblical times, he said.

The coronation was a theatrical performance as well, one that required costume changes. Victoria donned her state robes of satin and velvet and a red mantle

lined with ermine for the procession leading to the altar. When it was time for the archbishop to place the crown on her head, she changed into a linen sheath and gold tunic. The crown was new and adorned with rubies and sapphires pried from the one worn by her uncles George and William. That old crown was too large and stodgy for the petite young queen. The clergy also handed her the royal orb and scepter, precious symbols of enlightened rule.

Victoria stayed fresh and alert through the long ordeal. "Indeed," remarked the newspaper reporter, "as far as we could judge from her appearance and manner, we should say Her Majesty not only evinced the utmost coolness, composure, and command, but kept up, unflaggingly, an eager interest in the whole proceedings." She remained poised even when things went wrong, as they were bound to do. When the Archbishop of Canterbury went to place a ruby ring on her pinky, he pushed it onto the wrong finger, where it got stuck. Then, as the peers came forward to pay homage to her, one rickety lord stumbled on the steps leading to her chair. Victoria reached out a hand to help the aged man, and the congregation cheered.

At one festive point in the proceedings, the lord treasurer of the household tossed silver coronation medals into the lower galleries. Judges, noble lords, and privy councilors, keen to take home these keepsakes, "scrambled with the eagerness of children for sugar plums," said one observer. A son of the Duke of Richmond scooped up twelve medals, and the city's aldermen were nearly as quick. "Mr. Alderman Harmer was sprawling on the floor, and a struggle ensued between him and another person near him for one, which fell between them," Londoners read in their newspaper the next day. Things went smoothly after that until the Bishop of Bath and Wells declared the service over before it actually was. Victoria began to leave the church, only to be called back. Lord Melbourne watched the ceremony through tears of pride. "You did it beautifully—every part of it, with so much taste," he told Victoria. That night she stood on a balcony with her mother and Feodora and saw fireworks explode over Hyde Park in her honor.

People throughout Britain rejoiced; Reginamania was at its height; but things

happening behind palace walls would soon cause some of her subjects to hiss at Victoria in public. She had much to learn about being queen. She also lacked understanding that could only be gained through experience.

Trouble began the following winter, in January 1839, when Flora Hastings, one of the Duchess of Kent's ladies in waiting, developed pain and swelling in her abdomen. She went to see the royal physician, Sir James Clark. Hastings was wearing a corset and heavy skirt, which made undressing an ordeal. So instead of examining her, Clark advised Lady Flora to eat rhubarb and rest. He had no idea what was wrong with her, but the queen and Louise Lehzen put their heads together and came up with an explanation. As Victoria confided to her journal, "We have no doubt that she is—to use the plain words—*with child*!!" Because Hastings was unmarried, a pregnancy would be scandalous.

Victoria neither liked nor trusted Lady Flora, who was chummy with the Duchess of Kent and John Conroy. Hastings was a snoop, an "amazing spy who would repeat everything she heard," Victoria believed. Pretty soon her imagination took over, and not only was she sure Hastings was pregnant, but she suspected Conroy of being the baby's father.

The young queen whispered her allegations to her own ladies. A nasty rumor spread through Buckingham Palace, and eventually it reached Flora Hastings's ears. To save her reputation, Hastings insisted on being examined, however indelicate this might be. Dr.

Queen Victoria and Louise Lehzen distrusted Flora Hastings, a lady in waiting to the Duchess of Kent.

Queen Victoria receives the sacrament of
Communion during her coronation ceremony.

Clark and a colleague performed the exam with Hastings's maid and another lady present. Afterward, they issued their opinion. "Although there is an enlargement of the stomach," they stated, "there are no grounds for suspicion that pregnancy does exist, or ever did exist."

Victoria was filled with shame. To think that she had spread the awful lie! She went to see Hastings and embraced her. Grasping Hastings's hand, she apologized—almost. Without admitting her own role, she assured Lady Flora of her "great concern at what had happened" and her "wish that all should be forgotten." According to Victoria, Lady Flora "expressed herself exceedingly grateful to me, and said that, for Mama's sake, she would suppress every wounded feeling and would forget it."

But the Hastings family was less willing to forgive. Lady Flora's brother appealed to Lord Melbourne, demanding to know who was responsible for the campaign of whispers. Hastings's mother entreated Victoria to punish the gossipmongers. In her fury, she asked for Sir James Clark to be dismissed. If he had examined Lady Flora when she first consulted him, there would have been no ugliness to spread. The family did more: they leaked to the press letters on the sordid subject that had been exchanged between themselves and Lord Melbourne. The *Morning Post* even published a letter written by Flora Hastings herself stating that the rumor "was Her Majesty's own idea." In this way the scandal became public knowledge. People throughout England took sides, and most sympathized with Flora Hastings.

As the queen's popularity dwindled, so did her guilty feelings. She blamed the newspaper for the mess and "wished to have hanged the Editor and the whole Hastings family for their infamy." Lady Flora, she decided, was "such a nasty woman," whose belly, by the way, was continuing to swell.

Lady Flora was also growing weak and ill. Lord Melbourne tried to warn his queen that the lady might be dying, but Victoria refused to listen. It was just upset digestion, she told the prime minister. Or perhaps Hastings really was "with child" after all. Melbourne urged Victoria to see the ailing woman, but she was so annoyed

with the whole Hastings bunch that she went to a ball instead.

Melbourne was proven right on July 5, 1839, when Flora Hastings closed her eyes to the world. An autopsy revealed that she had a massive tumor on her liver. While others in the palace mourned, Victoria was still without remorse. She told Lord Melbourne, "I felt *I* had done nothing to kill her." Many Britons disagreed, believing that the queen's denial of comfort had hastened Lady Flora's death. Damning pamphlets appeared on the streets. "If one of the purest and fairest flowers of our British Nobility has been crushed by a most iniquitous and cruel blow, from the hand of power," read one, "the evidence

Sir James Clark served as a royal physician from 1837 until he retired in 1860.

is now before the Nation." People booed and shouted insults at Victoria when she attended the horseraces at Ascot that summer. Men failed to tip their hats to her.

Learning is sometimes painful. Victoria was discovering that as ruler she had to stay above rumors and petty squabbles. She needed to be thoughtful of others. She recalled words of encouragement from Feodora. "Living but for your duty to your country," Feodora had said, "difficult as it is, will prove to you a source of happiness few can know." Victoria could only hope this was true. She tried to make amends by sending fifty pounds to Lady Flora's maid, but her gift was returned. One day, while out walking with Lord Melbourne, she complained that a stone in her shoe was hurting her foot. It was her penance, Melbourne said.

Meanwhile, in May 1839, while the press was reporting on the Hastings

The queen and Lord Melbourne often went riding together.

scandal, Parliament took up the problem of cruel treatment of black workers in Jamaica, then a British colony. On August 1, 1838, African Jamaican workers had been granted full emancipation from slavery and forced apprenticeship. But the white planters who profited from their labor were ignoring the law. Melbourne wanted the government to take strong action, so he introduced a bill to suspend the Jamaican constitution and replace it with direct British rule. The Tories thought imposing direct rule was too extreme a move, and members of a smaller third party, the Radicals, agreed. As a result, the bill had less backing in the House of Commons than the prime minister had expected. It passed by five votes, which was hardly a majority at all. Melbourne foresaw that support for his government

and its policies would only continue to erode. He could no longer lead "with honour to myself, or with advantage to the country," he believed. Melbourne felt he had no choice but to resign and make way for a prime minister from the Tory Party.

He urged Victoria to accept the change "with that firmness which belongs to your character," but she took the news badly. "I really thought my heart would break!" she confessed. She pitied herself as "a poor helpless girl" who clung to the older man for protection and guidance. "The thought of ALL ALL my happiness being possibly at stake, so completely overcame me that I burst into tears and remained crying for some time," she said.

"You must try and be as collected as you can," Melbourne instructed. He advised her to send for the Duke of Wellington, who was an old and trusted Tory, and ask him to lead a new administration. Melbourne told Victoria that Wellington was likely to decline the prime minister's job because of his advanced age, but that he would probably suggest Sir Robert Peel, a younger man who was equally worthy.

In Victoria's opinion, Peel had peculiar ways of standing and moving and was too fond of his own cleverness. He spoke down to his queen, like a dancing master addressing a clumsy child. And his table manners were too, too vulgar! Victoria disliked him and hated to have him forced on her. "It is very hard, but it can't be helped" was all Melbourne would say.

After a night spent tossing and turning, Victoria saw the Duke of Wellington. As Lord Melbourne had predicted, the duke said that at age seventy, he was unsuited to lead his party. He recommended Sir Robert Peel.

Peel came to the palace that afternoon. "Such a cold, odd man," Victoria whispered to herself. Peel nervously thrust out his arms and pointed his toes this way and that. His strange mannerisms made Victoria feel ill at ease. But this conversation and another the next day went better than she had expected—until Peel brought up the queen's ladies of the bedchamber. They all had ties to the Whig party; a few were married to his staunch political enemies. She needed to replace some of the ladies with Tory women as a show of confidence, Peel said. He was

Sir Robert Peel shows off his pictures to guests. Peel's peculiar habits annoyed the queen.

going to have a tough enough time as it was, governing without a true majority in the House of Commons. People needed to know that the queen had faith in her prime minister and his party.

Victoria let him know that she intended to retain all her ladies. Not only did she never discuss politics with them, but the members of her household were her own affair. "I never saw a man so frightened," she noted with glee. "He was quite perturbed." The Duke of Wellington tried to persuade Victoria to change her mind, but she stood firm. "They wish to treat me like a girl, but I will show them I am Queen of England," she said, sounding exactly like a stubborn little girl.

People throughout England thought Victoria had acted foolishly. "She has made herself the Queen of a party," wrote Charles Greville in his journal. King Leopold's friend Baron Stockmar said that Melbourne and his ministers should have convinced Victoria to make the changes in her household that Peel had requested.

"How could they let the Queen make such mistakes, to the injury of the monarchy?" he asked.

In the end, because she refused to replace some of her ladies, the Tories declined to form a new government. Melbourne continued as prime minister, and the Whig government limped along. This was the outcome Victoria had wanted, and there were those who said she brought it about on purpose.

Victoria would deal with ten prime ministers, including Lord Melbourne, over the course of her long reign, each with his own talents and quirks. She would like one or two well enough to make them her friends, much like Melbourne. She would hate the very sight of another one, calling him "this half crazy & really in many ways ridiculous old man."

With time Britons forgot the "bedchamber crisis," as it came to be called, and even Flora Hastings. They grew to like Victoria again, but Reginamania was a thing of the past. Some people said it was high time for the queen to settle down and marry.

Queen Victoria would take a husband; of this there was no doubt. She was obligated to produce an heir, a son or daughter who would ascend to the throne upon her death. Also, marriage would put more distance between Victoria and the Duchess of Kent. Not only did the duchess still live with her, but etiquette required Victoria, as an unmarried lady, to have a chaperone when she ventured out. Too often, to Victoria's way of thinking, that chaperone was her mother.

Throughout history, England's monarchs rarely wed for love. Royal families married off their sons and daughters for strategic reasons: to strengthen their ties with other countries or enrich their treasuries. In 1501, Arthur Tudor, the oldest son of King Henry VII, was married to the Spanish princess Catherine of Aragon to firm up the alliance between England and Spain. After Arthur died in 1502, Catherine became the first wife of his younger brother, the future King Henry VIII.

In 1682, King George I married Sophia Dorothea of Celle, the daughter of a German duke, because she came with a hefty dowry and an ample yearly income.

Catherine of Aragon, the first wife of King Henry VIII, was queen of England
from 1509 until 1533, when Henry had the marriage declared invalid.
She was then banished from the royal court.

No law protected a wife's right to her money, so George was free to spend it as he chose. Husband and wife hated each other almost from the start, though. Sophia Dorothea bore two children, but after more than a decade of tantrums and angry scenes, the couple divorced. A sadder but wiser George I broke with tradition when he made sure that his son, the next King George, chose a wife he cared for.

Her subjects had been predicting whom Victoria would marry since she was nine years old. Some favored her cousin Prince George, the only son of her father's younger brother the Duke of Cumberland. (It was common for cousins to marry in nineteenth-century England.) Others rooted for a Frenchman, the Duke of Orléans; a Prussian, Prince Adelbert; or the future king of Denmark, Prince Christian. Many people hoped to see Victoria marry into the Dutch royal family. Indeed, a Dutch prince, a son of the Prince of Orange, had been the choice of the late king, William IV. William had even invited the Prince of Orange and his marriageable sons to England and introduced them to Victoria at a ball. But she found the lads to be dull-witted lumps of dough. "So much for the *Oranges,*" she wrote to her uncle Leopold.

It was fine with Leopold if his niece rejected the Dutch princes, because he secretly had other candidates in mind. He wanted Victoria to wed one of her Saxe-Coburg cousins, his nephews Ernst and Albert, to bolster that family's standing in Europe. As fortune would have it, the youths whose company Victoria had enjoyed in 1835 were planning a second trip to England.

TOO HAPPY!

VICTORIA COULD HARDLY wait for her cousins to come. "A young person like me must *sometimes* have young people to laugh with," she said. On October 10, 1839, the day Ernst and Albert were expected, she awoke with an aching head and a queasy stomach. She made herself get up and dress, and when informed that the princes had arrived, she waited at the top of a staircase to greet them.

One look was all she needed. Victoria's eyes met Albert's glance, and she fell passionately, profoundly in love. Albert was tall and slim. Everything about him was beautiful, Victoria thought. His manly build and his blue eyes started her heart "quite *going*." Since their last meeting, Albert had studied at Bonn University and toured Italy. He had grown curious about art, architecture, and the natural world. He liked to read and play sports.

Albert felt a strong attraction too. Within days Victoria confided in her journal, "Dearest Albert took my face in both his hands and kissed me most tenderly." In German he said, "I love you so much; I cannot tell you how much!" Albert was her "Dearest Angel," she wrote. "If I can only make *him* happy."

By 1839, Prince Albert was a trim, handsome young man.

Both were already thinking about marriage, but it was Victoria who raised the subject. Albert "would never have presumed to take such a liberty as to propose to the Queen of England," she was heard to say. So on October 15, shortly after noon, she summoned Albert for a private audience. Both were on edge, and a few minutes passed before Victoria found the courage to speak. She said that Albert must have known why she sent for him, that it would make her "too happy" if he consented to her wish that they marry.

Albert described what happened next in a letter to Baron Stockmar: "Victoria declared her love for me, and offered me her hand, which I seized in both of mine and pressed tenderly to my lips." Breaking the good news to her uncle Leopold, Victoria wrote, "Albert's *beauty is most striking,* and he is so amiable and unaffected—in short, very *fascinating.*" She insisted that Leopold keep the engagement secret for the time being.

In her diary Victoria expressed her joy fully, as she never could do in a letter to an uncle. "Oh! to feel I was, and am, loved by such an Angel as Albert was too great a delight to describe!" she wrote. "He is perfection; perfection in every way—in beauty—in everything!"

That night Albert had a nosebleed and went to bed early, but before retiring he handed Victoria a love letter. "Dearest, greatly beloved," she read in the privacy of her room. "How is it that I have deserved so much love, so much affection? I cannot get used to the reality of all that I see and hear. . . . Oh, that I may succeed in making you very, very happy, as happy as you deserve to be." Victoria shed tears of joy and fell asleep with Albert's words in her heart.

Because Victoria was queen, she and Albert enjoyed unusual freedom in becoming engaged. Typically, in the well-to-do families of nineteenth-century England, engagement followed a period of courtship that allowed a couple to get to know each other at dances and during closely supervised visits. A man then stood before a woman's parents or guardians and sought their approval to marry her. These elders had been observing his character throughout the couple's courtship. They

asked whether he had the means to provide and care for a wife. Both families considered finances—the gentleman's income and the lady's dowry—before the engagement proceeded. Victoria and Albert needed no one's permission, however. In fact, Victoria waited nearly a month, until it was almost time for Albert to leave, before breaking the news to her mother. The Duchess of Kent's feelings clearly were hurt and she cried as she embraced her daughter. She said that although she had not been consulted, she gave the couple her blessing and wished them happiness.

For a few delightful weeks the dreamy pair had sung duets at the piano, gone out riding together, stared into each other's eyes, and done lots of kissing. They sat "so nicely side by side on that little blue sofa," Victoria wrote. "He took my hands in his, and said my hands were so little he could hardly believe they were hands." When Victoria sat at her desk signing official papers, Albert stood beside her and applied a blotter to the wet ink of her signature. They gave each other rings and locks of hair, tokens of love to ease their loneliness after Albert returned to Coburg on November 14.

He sent her a letter from France as he made his way home. "All my thoughts have been with you," he wrote, but Albert had other matters on his mind. He had started to worry about being the husband of a powerful woman. Would he have important work of his own to do? He could never be happy if he was forced into idleness. Meanwhile, in England, Victoria attended to queenly business. After her midday meal on Saturday, November 23, she stood before a pair of folding doors at Buckingham Palace, waiting for them to be thrown open. She then swept into a room crowded with privy councilors. All could see by her flushed cheeks and bright eyes that she was excited. "The room was full, but I hardly knew who was there," Victoria admitted later. Wearing a bracelet containing a miniature portrait of Albert, she bowed to the gentlemen present. She sat down at the head of a long table and said, "Your Lordships will be seated." There were more councilors than chairs, so some sat while the rest stood.

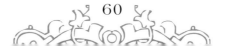

This cartoon likens Queen Victoria's betrothal to the leap-year tradition of women proposing marriage to men.

Her Majesty.   (——————) Duchess, of Kent. Duke, of Sussex.

The queen plays the piano, to the enjoyment of her gallant suitor and her devoted Dash. The Duchess of Kent and the Duke of Sussex, a younger brother of Victoria's father, chaperone the courting pair.

Victoria unfolded a piece of paper and read: "It is my intention to ally myself in marriage with Prince Albert of Saxe Coburg and Gotha." She added that she had come to this decision after "mature consideration." The marriage, she said, was "a matter so highly important to me and to my kingdom, and which I persuade myself will be most acceptable to all my loving subjects."

"Her hands trembled so excessively that I wonder she was able to read the paper which she held," remarked Charles Greville. "I felt my hands shook," Victoria

concurred, "but I did not make one mistake." She handed the paper, her official declaration of marriage, to one of the lords, who would have it published in the newspapers. "I felt most happy and thankful when it was over," Victoria said after leaving the room.

The news spread quickly. Everyone in England had an opinion about the match, and many people disliked it. Albert was twenty years old, like Victoria—too young to provide the guidance that a woman needed, some thought. "Were Prince Albert eight or ten years older, we should augur more confidently of the moral and political fruits to be anticipated from this alliance," wrote the editors of the *Times,* London's preeminent newspaper. Other people suspected Albert of marrying Victoria for money, knowing the Saxe-Coburg royals were far from rich. These lines flowed from one cruel, anonymous pen:

> *He comes to take "for better or worse"*
> *England's fat Queen and England's fatter purse.*

Lest he profit too much from Britain's wealth, Parliament voted to allow Albert thirty thousand pounds a year, less than he had expected. Two decades earlier, his uncle Leopold had been granted a fifty-thousand-pound allowance when he married Princess Charlotte.

Some critics questioned Albert's religion. By law, the queen could not marry a Roman Catholic, but in her declaration of marriage Victoria made no mention of Albert's faith. Tories still smarting over the bedchamber crisis raised suspicions that he was a Catholic, although they knew full well that he was a Protestant. "Do what one will, nothing will please these most religious, most hypocritical Tories," Victoria fumed. They were as bad as insects and turtle soup, two things she hated.

People also objected to Albert's being German. They pointed out that too many Germans had already married into the royal family, and Britain would gain nothing by adding another one. Among the German spouses they counted on their fingers

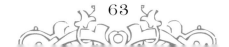

were Leopold, Queen Adelaide (the wife of William IV), and Victoria's own mother, the Duchess of Kent. Even Lord Melbourne thought, "We have Coburgs enough." (Victoria consulted Melbourne on most matters, but not about her marriage.)

Albert's most vocal critic was the Duke of Wellington. Victoria was so peeved at the old Tory that she threatened not to invite him to her wedding. Lord Melbourne reminded her that Wellington was a national hero and an elder statesman. It would never do to snub him. "It is MY marriage and I will only have those who can sympathise with me," she countered. She remained so stubbornly against Wellington that Melbourne and Charles Greville had to plead with her to send the old man a note when he got sick.

Despite their misgivings, Lord Melbourne and everyone else in Britain put on a good face as the wedding date approached, and welcomed Albert to his new home. On February 7, 1840, he arrived in England, accompanied by his father and brother. They had endured a rough voyage; a winter storm blew over the English Channel, tossing the ship and making them all seasick. "I never remember having suffered so long or so violently," Albert told Victoria. "When we landed our faces were more the colour of wax candles than human visages." Although chilly rain fell when Albert stepped ashore at Dover, on England's southern coast, thousands turned out to cheer him. A cavalry regiment, the Eleventh Light Dragoons, escorted his party through the streets of the county of Kent as they made their way to London. From that day on, this army unit would be known as Prince Albert's Own Hussars.

Victoria worried about Albert while he was traveling and watched for his arrival from a window of Buckingham Palace. When his carriage at last drove up late in the afternoon, she hurried to the door to embrace him. "Seeing his *dear dear* face again put me at rest about everything," she sighed. Very soon they would be husband and wife.

The wedding was going to be lavish. Victoria had wanted a small, intimate affair, but Lord Melbourne insisted it be splashy and splendid and costly. After all, a reigning queen of England had not taken a husband since 1554, when Mary I—the

The vessel carrying Prince Albert to England tosses on a stormy sea before docking at Dover.

ruthless ruler known as Bloody Mary—married Philip of Spain. Victoria grumbled that "everything was always made so uncomfortable for Kings and Queens." But she took out her pencils and designed herself a wedding gown with a low, scooped neckline, short, ruffled sleeves, and a train six yards long.

Two hundred women made lace for the dress. When their work was complete, they destroyed the pattern so it could never be copied. Victoria also designed a dress for her twelve bridesmaids, as well as the golden brooches that she would give them as keepsakes. The brooches were all alike, shaped like an eagle and encrusted with diamonds, rubies, turquoise, and pearls.

Lord Melbourne never doubted that a large royal wedding would thrill the public, even though many Britons were poor, hungry, and cold. The Industrial Revolution that had brought wealth to middle-class factory owners and merchants had devastated places where artisans earned a living with their hands. One such spot was Spitalfields, on the outskirts of London, where generations of weavers had produced silk cloth on home looms. By the 1830s, machines had taken over the work of

Crowding, hunger, and filth were a way of life in nineteenth-century London slums.

weaving, and Spitalfields suffered. "The low houses are all huddled together in close and dark lanes and alleys" and "falling for want of repair," noticed one well-off person who went walking there. So many doors and windows had been broken that the observer had trouble believing anyone lived behind them. Yet "in every room of these houses, whole families, parents, children, and aged grandfathers swarm together," he knew. Black mud and filth filled the unpaved streets, where the stench of rotting animal carcasses and vegetables made the air unbreathable.

A law passed in 1834 required the neediest people—the desperate ones who turned to society for aid—to enter workhouses. A workhouse offered food, clothing, and shelter in exchange for manual labor. Girls and women cleaned, cooked, and did laundry for the whole institution. Men might break stones for road building or crush animal bones for fertilizer. Life inside was so harsh that it felt to the poor more like punishment than help. People slept in crowded dormitories, and they were likely to find rat droppings or dead beetles in their meager food. In 1836, four of every ten people living in British workhouses were children. Some orphaned and abandoned youngsters spent sixteen years behind workhouse walls.

Victoria had glimpsed poverty eight years earlier, as a child riding through Wales. Since then, she had inhabited a world of manicured gardens, satin gowns, and formal receptions under twinkling chandeliers. Once she became queen, Lord

Melbourne shielded her from want and distress. As a Whig he was happy to extend voting rights to some property owners, but he felt less generous toward paupers. He freely admitted that he disliked them: "Those who are poor through their own fault, I quite detest," he said. Like many people of his time, he believed the poor were lazy, dishonest, and drunk. In 1839, when Victoria told Melbourne that the poverty depicted in Charles Dickens's new novel, *Oliver Twist,* made her sad, he dismissed her feelings. "I don't like these things; I wish to avoid them," he told the queen. "I don't like them in *reality* and therefore I don't wish to see them represented." Victoria would be wise, he implied, to shut them out of her mind as well.

Many people slept in the same workhouse room.

"Please, sir, I want some more." Oliver pleads for a second bowl of gruel for himself and the other starving workhouse boys in an illustration from Charles Dickens's *Oliver Twist*.

There was hardly an unpleasant thought in the neighborhood of Buckingham Palace on the morning of February 10, 1840. It was the day of Her Majesty's wedding. Despite rain and wind, by nine o'clock her joyous subjects were thronging the streets. They were eager to see the royal procession make its way to the chapel at St. James's Palace, where the noon nuptials would take place. Enterprising citizens sold space on chairs, tables, and benches. For a few shillings, a person could stand on a piece of furniture and look over the heads of others. Some brave souls scrambled into trees to get a better view for free. Here and there a branch gave way, causing startled climbers to tumble. "Many of them excited roars of laughter," the press reported, and no one was hurt. All the while, local butchers kept up a clattering serenade on the marrowbone and cleaver. This was in keeping with the century-old tradition of English butchers' saluting a bride and groom by striking a hefty bone against their big meat cutters.

Soon enough, the procession of carriages began. The ladies' dresses were of "every known colour," noted the *Times*. Pastel blue and green, two popular hues, were intermingled with "amber, crimson, purple, fawn, stone, and a considerable number of white robes." Black suits for men had been banished in favor of lighter shades.

People cheered when they spotted a famous face. The Duke of Wellington gave a slight nod to the hurrahs that greeted him; he had been invited after all. Applause rang out for Prince Albert, who wore the gold-trimmed red coat of a British field marshal. "Every sympathy was awakened on behalf of her Royal Highness the Duchess of Kent," the *Times* reported, "but she appeared somewhat disconsolate and distressed." The duchess had wanted a more prestigious place in the procession. She made sure everyone saw that she was miffed. The public recognized Victoria's father's younger brother the Duke of Sussex, who would give away the bride, and Lord Melbourne, who carried the sword of state. At last came the queen, looking pale but lovely behind the lace veil that draped her face. She wore a wreath of orange blossoms and a diamond and sapphire brooch that was a gift from Albert.

Inside the Royal Chapel, the bridesmaids in their simple dresses and white roses "looked like village girls, among all the gorgeous colours and jewels that surrounded them," commented one of the queen's ladies in waiting. The train of Victoria's gown was too short for twelve bridesmaids to carry easily. "We were all huddled together, and scrambled rather than walked along, kicking each other's heels and treading on each other's gowns," said one. The lady in waiting observed, "The Queen's look and manner were very pleasing; her eyes much swoln with tears, but great happiness in her face." Both Victoria and Albert trembled a little, as young brides and grooms often do. They exchanged their vows, and when they found a few minutes alone, they promised never to keep secrets from each other.

There was a wedding breakfast at Buckingham Palace at two that afternoon.

Following pages: Sunlight filters through a chapel window and falls on Queen Victoria and Prince Albert as they exchange marriage vows.

Four servants carried in the wedding cake, which measured nine feet around and weighed three hundred pounds. Sculpted figures atop it represented Britannia, a mythical woman who stood for Great Britain, smiling down on Victoria and Albert, who were dressed in Grecian robes.

The day's excitement left Victoria with a headache. She began her three-day honeymoon at Windsor lying on a sofa while Albert played soothing melodies on a piano. "Ill or not, I *never, never* spent such an evening," Victoria confided in her journal. To be called tender names was "bliss beyond belief!" she wrote. "Oh! this was the happiest day of my life!"

CHAPTER V

PRINCE VERSUS QUEEN

THREE DAYS! ALBERT had hoped for a traditional honeymoon: a month, six weeks, or more away from prying eyes and familiar scenes. He longed for quiet time alone with Victoria, a chance for them to get used to married life. Albert and Victoria had fallen in love and pledged to spend their lives together so quickly. In many ways they were strangers to each other, as Albert was finding out. Please, he asked his bride, could they escape for "at least a fortnight—or a week"?

"You forget, my dearest Love," Victoria replied, "that I am the Sovereign, and that business can stop and wait for nothing." Parliament was in session; she could spend a few days, at most, away from London.

Albert could see that she missed city life. He liked country living and early bedtimes, but Victoria thrived in company and could happily dance past midnight. She even danced at a ball while on her honeymoon, which straight-laced Albert thought improper. Another husband might have forbidden his new wife from displaying herself in this way, but Victoria was queen of England and could do as she wished. "I am only the husband," Albert said, "and not the master in the house."

Victoria drew this sketch of her beloved Albert. When they married, Victoria was a queen, but Albert did not become king. In 1857 Victoria bestowed on him the title prince consort, indicating that he was married to the reigning British queen.

Once the brief honeymoon was over and the couple returned to palace life, the daily routine left Albert lonely and bored. His friends were all in Germany; speaking English felt strange. Worst of all, he had nothing to do. He had expected to be Victoria's advisor and helpmate, but she shut him out of her work. "The English are very jealous of any foreigner interfering in the government of this country," she told him as an excuse. "I am certain you will understand this, but it is much better not to say anything more about it now." Albert did not understand, and he did say more. In fact, the couple had noisy arguments about his role. In his angriest moments he told himself that Victoria's naturally fine character had been "warped in many respects by wrong upbringing."

Nevertheless, there were enough joyful, carefree, passionate times to make Victoria feel dismayed when she quickly became pregnant. She expected to have children one day, but this was way too soon. She and Albert would never again be young newlyweds without the worries of a family. She had hoped to linger in the sweetness of new love. "I prayed God night and day to be left free for at least six months, but my prayers have not been answered," Victoria wrote. Prayer was the only birth control method she knew.

The pregnancy delighted Albert. Not only did he looked forward to fatherhood, but the coming of a child meant that his role was about to change. The little prince

In a happy moment, the newlyweds enjoy a glide on the ice.

or princess would be heir to the British throne. If Victoria should die before the boy or girl came of age, then Parliament would appoint a regent, most likely the child's father. Albert and Victoria hoped he would never have to step into that role, but they wanted him to be prepared. Albert had his desk moved next to Victoria's so he could study the official papers that required her attention. He sat beside her as she opened Parliament that fall.

He made his first public appearance on June 1, when he chaired a meeting of the Society for the Extinction of the Slave Trade. Most European nations and the United States had outlawed the capture and shipping of Africans, but the practice continued, often illegally. Albert expressed his hope that "the benevolent and persevering exertions of England" would soon end a practice that was "at once the desolation of Africa and the blackest stain upon civilized Europe." Three times the audience interrupted his speech with cheers and tremendous applause.

Nine days later, the prince showed that he could keep his head in the face of danger. The threat appeared suddenly, when he and Victoria went out for a ride in an open carriage. It was six o'clock in the evening at a time of year when days were long in England and the sun shone into the night. The greenery in Hyde Park glowed softly. People were out savoring this beautiful hour and hoping to glimpse the royal couple. This was why the man in worn clothing leaning against a nearby rail caused no concern—at first.

He was a "small, disagreeable looking man," Albert saw. The fellow held something; Albert could not tell what it was. But it was a pistol, which he aimed at the queen and fired. Luckily, he missed Victoria, who had been looking at something else. She wondered at the loud crack and asked herself, Could someone be shooting birds in Hyde Park? She turned as Albert began to jump from the carriage to go after the would-be assassin. Seeing that the man held a second pistol, Victoria pulled her husband back and crouched with him on the carriage floor. "If it please Providence I shall escape," she prayed. The shooter's next shot also missed its

target. By this time brave bystanders had rushed to the scene, and they overcame the man.

Victoria and Albert were close to home and could easily have retreated, but Albert ordered the carriage to drive on. He thought it was important to show Victoria's subjects that he and the queen felt safe among them. The couple drove through the streets for an hour, past waving hats and cheers. They paid a call on the Duchess of Kent, who had rented a house on fashionable Belgrade Square. When they returned to the palace, a crowd greeted them with "long and loud huzzahs," according to a press report. Only when they were at last alone did Victoria and Albert let their emotions flow. She cried, and he held her close and kissed her.

Anyone could see that Albert had a fine, upstanding character. He spoke with intelligence and carried himself well. People in England forgot all about his youth and German heritage. They dismissed any lingering doubts about his religion. It was "now all the fashion to praise Prince Albert," said Lord Holland, an aging Whig.

Albert took Victoria's place at Privy Council meetings as her pregnancy progressed. He chaired a commission to promote the fine arts. "I have my hands very full," he proudly informed his brother. Albert also oversaw long-needed improvements to damp, drafty, smelly old Buckingham Palace. For the first time since Victoria made the palace her home, water flowed through all the pipes, and the kitchen and lavatories could be aired out.

The prince also brought efficiency to a wasteful royal household that had too many servants. One servant laid the wood in fireplaces, but another came in to light it. There was one to wash windows on the inside, and another to wash them on the outside. If one of those windows broke, six separate household officials had to sign the authorization to have it replaced. As a result, windows often stayed broken, and rain soaked priceless antique furniture. The servants answered to different bosses, who paid little attention to what they did. This meant that work went undone and supplies disappeared. Yet the staff suffered no consequences and was

This picture was presented as an accurate depiction of the shooting incident. The would-be assassin was Edward Oxford, an unemployed waiter. He was tried and found not guilty by reason of insanity and sentenced to the State Criminal Lunatic Asylum. After twenty-four years he was allowed to immigrate to Australia. Oxford's was the first of seven attempts made on Queen Victoria's life during her long reign. The shooters all displayed mental instability, although some were also politically motivated.

highly paid. When a typical household servant earned twelve pounds a year, those at Buckingham Palace received sixty pounds, a hundred forty pounds, or more. They pocketed hefty tips from foreign guests, and they looked forward to ample pensions when they retired.

Albert fired the extra workers. He placed those who remained under the watchful eye of one trustworthy senior servant. He put an end to wasteful work, such as the daily replacement of candles throughout the palace. He saved the government twenty-five thousand pounds a year and turned the palace into a model of order and efficiency.

The prince had carved out a role for himself. He explained to the Duke of Wellington that as Victoria's husband he ought to be "the natural head of the family, superintendent of her household, manager of her private affairs, her sole *confidential* advisor in politics, and only assistance in her communications with the officers of the Government."

Albert urged his pregnant wife to rest as her December due date neared, but Victoria felt too strong and healthy to stay still. "I am wonderfully well," she wrote to Feodora. "I take long walks, some in the highest wind, every day, and am so active, though of a *great* size, I must unhappily admit."

The baby arrived two weeks early, on November 22, 1840, a rainy, windy day when fires had been lit throughout the palace to chase away the chill. The royal couple welcomed a daughter, a princess named Victoria Adelaide Mary Louisa.

Like other well-to-do Englishwomen, Queen Victoria rested for two full weeks after giving birth. Albert's care of her "was like that of a mother," she informed her actual mother, the Duchess of Kent. "Nor could there be a kinder, wiser, or more judicious nurse," she added. If Victoria grew weary of lying in bed, Albert carried her to a sofa. He wrote letters for her, and he read to her while she lay back and closed her eyes.

Upper-class children, even babies, spent most of their time away from their parents, cared for by nannies and nursemaids. The royal couple placed a woman

named Mrs. Southey in charge of their nursery. Mrs. Southey was old and wore a wig that had been fashionable in the last century, but the Archbishop of Canterbury had recommended her. They hired a wet nurse—a lactating woman—to breastfeed the little princess, whom they called Vicky. Maids bathed and dressed the infant and brought her to see her mother twice a day. Victoria's love for her daughter blossomed. "She has big dark blue eyes and a beautiful complexion," Victoria bragged. By the time Vicky was christened, on her parents' first anniversary, the queen was pregnant again.

The year 1841 brought another change, one Victoria had dreaded. That summer the nation held a general election, and the Tories won an unmistakable victory. Lord Melbourne's years as prime minister were over; this time the queen could do nothing to keep him in office. "*Eleven days* was the *longest* I was ever without seeing him," she reflected.

Melbourne had been her teacher, guide, and valued friend while she grew into the role of queen. The two would never be so close again. Melbourne promised to write to Victoria, but never about official matters. He told her he was tired and ready for a rest, and he reminded her that she had another capable advisor, her husband. "The Prince understands everything so well, and has a clever able head," he said.

There was no fit of crying when Lord Melbourne took his leave. But the new prime minister was Sir Robert Peel, the man Victoria sent cowering two years before, when she refused to replace some of her ladies. People who watched the goings-on in government held their breath: How would Peel and the queen get along this time? "She would like him better if he would keep his legs still," the diary writer Charles Greville thought.

Both Victoria and Peel were relieved to find that they could work together without friction. Peel assured the queen that it would be his "first and greatest duty to consult her happiness and comfort." When Charles Greville asked him how their first meeting went, Peel replied, "Perfectly." Greville noted, "In short, he was more than satisfied; he was charmed with her." Peel was pleased with Victoria's

As her proud parents look on, Princess Victoria is christened by the Archbishop of Canterbury. The Duke of Wellington stands prominently to the left.

Queen Victoria and her second prime minister, Sir Robert Peel, formed a good working relationship despite early differences. Peel died unexpectedly on July 2, 1850, of injuries received when he fell from a horse.

new willingness to replace some of her ladies with Tory women. Tories, Whigs—such distinctions mattered less, Victoria observed, "when one is so happy, blessed in one's home life."

On November 9, 1841, with Vicky not quite a year old, Victoria gave birth to a big, robust prince. His parents named him Albert Edward, after his father and his late grandfather, the Duke of Kent. The infant boy was given the title Prince of Wales, signifying that he was heir of the reigning British monarch. The rules of succession that were followed at the time favored men and boys. The prince stood next in line to the throne, followed by his older sister. Any more boys born to Victoria and Albert would stand ahead of Vicky as well.

Euphoria spread through the nation along with word of the baby's birth. As cannons boomed, people spilled into the streets to sing "God Save the Queen," the British national anthem. From her resting place Victoria heard the cheers erupting outside Buckingham Palace.

The *Times* marveled at the "one universal feeling of joy throughout the kingdom." The paper's ecstatic editors praised Victoria's kindness, purity, and graciousness. In her government dealings she was ever impartial, they stated clearly they chose to overlook the recent past. Albert, they said, possessed "rare and admirable virtues," such as "high cultivation of mind" and "accomplished taste." The royal couple, so devoted to family, were "the model of their own generation."

At age twenty-two Queen Victoria was already the mother of a girl and a boy.

Yet at home the model pair was quarreling again, this time about Louise Lehzen. Victoria's old governess had been jealous of Albert from the moment he took his place at the queen's side, and he resented her too. Albert was sure Lehzen had persuaded Victoria to shut him out of her official life in the first months of the marriage. Too often, it seemed to Albert, when he and Victoria were sketching together or playing duets on the piano, Lehzen would appear. She would drag Victoria away to see to some household matter that she claimed could not wait. What was more, she still slept in a room with a door that opened into the queen's bedchamber. (It was common in nineteenth-century England for a husband and wife to have separate bedrooms.) Albert hated the woman and called her an old hag. He detested the odor that enveloped her like smog, that of the caraway seeds Lehzen chewed constantly to control her intestinal gas.

Lehzen had been a loyal, loving caregiver during the years John Conroy preyed on Victoria, years when Albert was far away. It was hard for him to understand that she had earned the queen's lasting affection. To him the old governess was an enemy. He maintained, "There can be no improvement until Victoria sees Lehzen as she is."

When Albert finally lost his temper over Lehzen, he was really upset about something else: the health of Vicky, the princess royal. The Prince of Wales—little Prince "Bertie"—was thriving; he cooed and smiled and never had colic. But Vicky was puny and ill. Something had to be very wrong in the nursery. It hardly mattered that two babies were too much for the ancient Mrs. Southey to handle, or that Dr. Clark had dosed the little girl with calomel, a toxic mercury compound. Albert was sure Lehzen had caused Vicky's illness by sticking her nose where it didn't belong. He had no evidence, but he had seen her gossiping with Mrs. Southey. He came to a decision: Baroness Lehzen had to go.

Discussing the matter with his wife was impossible. "She will not hear me out but flies into a rage and overwhelms me with reproaches of suspiciousness,

want of trust, ambition, envy, etc. etc.," Albert complained to Baron Stockmar, the longtime family friend. Victoria's loved ones knew she had a quick temper, but she was also affected by the devastating sadness and unsteady emotions that some women experience after giving birth. Today doctors call this condition postpartum depression.

Victoria could be stubborn and volatile, but so could Albert. The dispute got worse and worse. Before long, the two were avoiding each other altogether. Instead of speaking, they communicated through Stockmar. In one of his angriest moments Albert wrote a spiteful letter to Victoria that he asked the baron to deliver. "Take the child away and do as you like and if she dies you will have it on your conscience," he wrote.

Rather than give Victoria this awful letter, Stockmar offered her advice. If the terrible fight continued, the marriage would be damaged beyond repair, he warned. Albert might even leave England. Immediately Victoria understood that the argument had spun out of control, and that she was partly to blame. "Albert must tell me what he dislikes and I will set about to remedy it," she told the baron. "When I am in a passion which I trust I am not very often in now, he must not believe the stupid things I say."

The whole deplorable mess forced Victoria to be honest about her temper. "There is often an irritability in me," she saw, "but I will strive to conquer it though I knew *before* I was married that this would be a trouble." She would be wise to give in, in the current situation, so she agreed with Albert to let Lehzen go.

The baroness was to take a six-month rest because of her health—this was the official story. The queen, Albert, and Lehzen all understood, though, that she was departing for good. She was given a generous yearly pension of eight hundred pounds, and in September 1842 she left for Germany, where she would live with her sister. She declined to take leave of Victoria in person and sent her a letter instead. "It was very painful to me waking this morning," Victoria said the next day, "and

Sarah Spencer, Lady Lyttelton, brought experience and common sense into the royal nursery.

recollecting she was really quite away. I had been dreaming she had come back to say good-bye to me."

Mrs. Southey also left, and willingly. "No bird can return more eagerly to her nest than I to my own home," she said. Victoria and Albert asked one of the queen's ladies of the bedchamber to take over the nursery. Lady Sarah Lyttelton was a widow of fifty-five with grown children. She was a practical woman with a sense of humor who admired Prince Albert. She agreed to enforce the nursery rules that the children's parents had put in place: Vicky and Bertie were never to be left alone; no unauthorized person was allowed to see them; Victoria and Albert were to be informed of their progress and any change in their daily activities.

She also laid down rules of her own, because the children were being "over-watched and over-doctored," as she put it. She was to have complete charge of the nursery. She wanted the right to ask questions of the queen and prince and to discuss the children's care freely and openly with them. If Victoria or Albert had cause to reprimand her, they were to do so privately. She wanted to be present at the children's medical exams, and, finally, she would select their clothing. How could Princess Vicky run and tumble, dressed up as she was in "garter-blue velvet, Brussels lace, white shoes, pearls and diamonds"? Children needed play clothes.

Eager for competent care of their children, Victoria and Albert consented to Lyttelton's terms. Soon, as Vicky grew round and rosy, Victoria could write in her journal, "Nothing could go on better, than does the Nursery. Lady Lyttelton is of course perfection." And the queen and prince were enjoying some peace. They were learning that a successful marriage requires compromise.

CHAPTER VI

FAMILY LIFE

VICTORIA AND ALBERT'S third child, Princess Alice, was born in April 1843. In September, the queen and prince consort sailed to France on the royal yacht. They were to be guests of the French king, Louis Philippe, and the queen consort, Marie Amélie. It was Victoria's first trip outside Britain, and it was historic. An English monarch had not set foot on French soil since 1520, when King Henry VIII went to France in a gesture of friendship. Statesmen on both sides of the English Channel hoped the visit would strengthen the bond between the two nations. The queen and Prince Albert had left their children in the safety of Lady Lyttelton's care, but Victoria said she felt "agitated" when away from them.

Albert was seasick during the voyage, but Victoria loved bounding over the waves. She stood at the rail and faced into the wind, savoring what she called "the sailor-gypsy life." As the yacht neared land, she saw that a crowd had turned out to greet the royal visitors. People shouted, *Vive la reine d'Angleterre!* Long live the queen of England!

Upon stepping ashore, Victoria and Albert crowded into an old carriage with

the French king and queen and several of their grown children. The route to their hosts' summer residence, in the town of Eu, took them over dusty, rocky, rutted country roads. At one treacherous spot, the clumsy coach nearly toppled over. But the royal travelers safely reached the Château d'Eu, which was an enormous palace of brick and stone built in the 1400s. In the square courtyard before the entrance, a French military band played "God Save the Queen."

Louis Philippe and Marie Amélie were warm, gracious hosts. "The whole family received us with a heartiness, I might say affection, which was quite touching," Albert said. Victoria was "as amused as a child could be, and very much pleased

Lady Charlotte Canning painted this watercolor picture of the royal party arriving at the Château d'Eu.

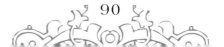

with her reception," noted the lady in waiting who accompanied her, Charlotte Canning. "Louis-Philippe tells her over & over again how enchanted he is with this visit." At age sixty-nine the French king was a jowly man with a round belly. He had puffs of whiskers on his cheeks and a pile of dark curls on top of his head. He was mild-tempered, ever polite, and good at making small talk. He kept to a daily routine that he expected his family and guests to follow. It began at seven thirty a.m. with a heavy breakfast of soup, sausages, eggs, and sweet rolls.

Born a duke's son, Louis Philippe was a teenager in 1789, when a peasant uprising swelled into a revolution that swept through France. It led to the beheading of his distant cousin King Louis XVI, Queen Marie Antoinette, and thousands of nobles, including his father. His surviving family fled and watched from a distance as France endured years of instability. In 1804 the military leader Napoleon Bonaparte proclaimed himself emperor and began a campaign to conquer Europe. After Great Britain and other powers defeated Napoleon in 1815, France reinstated its monarchy. Louis Philippe, a popular figure, was made king in 1830.

Marie Amélie was an Italian princess when Louis Philippe met her. She had a long face that looked dour in portraits, but in her company Victoria was "very merry and laughed a good deal." Marie Amélie had been a devoted mother to her ten children, six of whom were still living. One was Queen Louise of Belgium, wife of Victoria's uncle Leopold.

Louis Philippe lived during a tumultuous time in French history. He was proclaimed king in 1830, at age fifty-six.

Queen Victoria liked Queen Marie Amélie's sprightly nature.

"I feel so gay and happy with these dear people," Victoria wrote in her journal. During their five days in Eu, Victoria and Albert were treated to grand dinners with forty or more guests, and sumptuous picnics in the forest. Musicians entertained, among them a man who played three notes at once on a French horn. "Somehow it was not pretty," Lady Canning stated. "The poor performer's sounds became stranger & stranger." One duke started giggling, and soon the whole audience was shaking with stifled laughter. Canning felt "very sorry for the man, but his back was partly turned & I hope he did not find out."

After a brief return to England to see their children and be assured that they were well, Victoria and Albert spent a few days in Belgium with King Leopold and Queen Louise. As they toured Brussels and other Belgian cities, Victoria's wardrobe attracted notice that made her lady in waiting cringe. All her clothes were "decidedly very badly chosen, and quite unlike what she ought to have," in Charlotte Canning's opinion. Anyone could see that the queen's black silk gown, newly arrived from Paris, had been fitted to her body hastily and sloppily. The bonnet she wore in the city of Ghent, said Canning, "would do for an old woman of seventy." In France she had appeared at a party in a purplish-brown silk dress, yellow bonnet adorned with flowers, and black lace shawl.

Victoria may have lacked fashion sense, but she thoroughly enjoyed her time in Belgium. Thanking her uncle and aunt for their kindness, she wrote, "The stay was *so delightful,* but so painfully short!" It had been pure joy, she added, to sleep "under the roof of one who has ever been a father to me."

She and Albert longed for a place of their own where they could escape from London and the pomp of palace life. They wanted a spot where they could simply be parents and enjoy their growing brood. Brighton Pavilion, the domed palace built by George IV, was too much of a "strange Chinese thing, haunted by ghosts best forgotten," Victoria commented. Besides, the town of Brighton had been built up all around it, allowing the family no privacy. Victoria would sell Brighton Pavilion in 1850.

She and Albert found what they were looking for on the Isle of Wight, the southern island Victoria had visited as a child, when she and her mother stayed in Norris Castle. A writer in the early 1800s described the isle as "all that is grand and lovely in England"—in miniature. It offered quaint villages, gentle rivers, forests, farms, and flower-blanketed vales. A chalk ridge running along its coastline reminded many people of the famed white cliffs at Dover. Victoria and Albert bought an estate on the island called Osborne, which came complete with a house, hundreds of acres of parkland, and a private beach.

"It is impossible to see a prettier place," Victoria informed Lord Melbourne, but Albert was already planning big changes. He thought the house, with sitting rooms and sixteen bedrooms on the first two floors, was too small. A royal residence needed chambers large enough for gatherings of the Privy Council, because the queen never traveled to meet with her ministers; they went to her. So Albert had the house torn down. He then set to work designing a larger one and having it built. The project filled him with energy. "I, partly forester, partly builder, partly farmer, and partly gardener, expect to be a good deal upon my legs and in the open air," he said.

The new house was Albert's version of an Italian villa, because the serene, blue sea around the island made him think of Naples, where he had traveled before his marriage. It had two towers and a separate wing for the Duchess of Kent to use

Following pages: An informal gathering at the Château d'Eu: to the left, Prince Albert and King Louis Philippe share a sofa. Queen Victoria and Queen Marie Amélie sit next to each other at the table.

Osborne House, on the Isle of Wight, became the royal family's private retreat.

when she came to stay. It was also the first royal residence to have flushing toilets. Outdoors, a tree-lined avenue led to the entrance of the new Osborne House, and fountains splashed beneath its windows.

Osborne House was cheerful and unlike a palace in Victoria's eyes; it was just what she had wanted. It was where she felt most at home, according to Baron von Bunsen, the Prussian ambassador to Great Britain, who visited Osborne: "She there enjoys her domestic life and family happiness to her heart's content. She walks out in the beautiful gardens and pleasure-grounds with the Prince and her children, in prospect of the sea."

Victoria called her children a blessing, but she rarely kissed and cuddled them. Instead she showed her love by worrying and scolding. Weighed down by pregnancy throughout the 1840s, she seldom joined the youngsters in spontaneous

Queen Victoria and her family celebrate Christmas. Decorating a tree was a German holiday tradition that the queen and Prince Albert made popular in England.

play. The queen gave birth to a son, Prince Alfred, in August 1844. A fifth child, Princess Helena, was born in 1846. Princess Louise was born in 1848, and Prince Arthur followed in 1850. To be repeatedly pregnant and giving birth, as so many married women were in the nineteenth century, was "not very nice," Victoria said. It made her feel "more like a rabbit or guinea-pig than anything else." She believed that Albert, like all men, had no understanding of the physical ordeal that married women went through. Still, there were times, especially at Osborne, when Victoria danced with the children or ventured out with them at night to catch moths.

Albert could be a different kind of parent. He played boisterous, giggling games of hide-and-seek with his sons and daughters. In summer he rolled with them on the grass, and in winter he led them in building lofty snowmen. He helped them put on plays to entertain their mother. At Osborne, he taught the children to plant and care for flowers and vegetables. Albert and the boys built a miniature cottage on the estate grounds. It contained a small kitchen, where the girls learned to cook, and space for the children to display their collections of butterflies, pressed flowers, and seashells.

"He is so kind to them and romps with them so delightfully, and manages them so beautifully and firmly," Victoria wrote in her journal. Albert could also be more than firm, since he believed in harsh punishments. Disobedient princes and princesses received whippings or were forced to stand for long periods with their hands tied together. Princess Alice was whipped for fibbing when she was only four years old.

Whether at Osborne House or Buckingham Palace, Queen Victoria took pride in her family, believing that she, Albert, and the children set a high moral standard for the nation. "They say, no Sovereign was ever more loved than I am (I am bold enough to say)," she wrote to her uncle Leopold, "& *this* because of our happy domestic home, and the good example it presents."

Victoria had more on her mind than home and family. She had 156 million subjects, according to the latest calculation, living in Great Britain or in its colonies

The queen and prince consort are shown playing with their children.

around the world. They all counted on her to have their interests at heart. Her government expected her to stay informed about happenings at home and abroad, and to promote British interests and achievements.

The role of queen came with responsibilities—and with risks. On April 8, 1848, the day Princess Louise turned three weeks old, Queen Victoria, Prince Albert, and their children hurriedly boarded a train. It carried them away from London, where Louise was born, at an astonishing thirty miles per hour—three times the speed of a horse-drawn coach. The family headed south toward Osborne House, because the capital had grown unsafe for them. The threat came from some of the queen's own subjects, protesters who called themselves Chartists.

Anger had been building among working-class Britons for years. The winter of 1837–38—the first winter of Victoria's reign—had been unusually harsh. Its bitter temperatures harmed the wheat crop. A poor harvest, coupled with tariffs on imported grain, made bread more costly. Prices remained high into the 1840s, creating hardship for workers in towns and cities. They had no way to grow their own food and struggled to feed their families. With many of the poor forced to enter workhouses, some laborers started to think that they were entitled to better. As one man wrote, "Hungry in a land of plenty, I began seriously for the first time in my life to enquire WHY, WHY."

The Chartists believed that with a voice in government, they could get laws passed to improve their lives. They drafted a charter, or petition, demanding their rights as citizens. These included the rights to vote and run for Parliament, whether or not they owned property. The Chartists announced that on April 10, 1848, they would gather in London by the hundreds of thousands. They were going to march on Parliament and present the House of Commons with their charter, which bore more than five million signatures—or so they claimed.

Would violence break out? London had cause to be afraid. In France, widening poverty and hunger had led to an uprising known as the Revolution of 1848. Louis

Philippe, once a popular king, was forced to abdicate. Disguised in rough workers' clothes, he and Queen Marie Amélie fled France in a fishing boat as French voters elected Louis Napoleon, nephew of the emperor Napoleon, to be their president. Other parts of Europe were witnessing social unrest as well. "European war is at our doors," Albert feared.

Some Chartists were peaceful men who simply wanted to exercise their constitutional right to present a petition to Parliament. Others, however, were eager to fight for change. The royal family had a preview of their tactics in March, when an angry mob broke windows at the Duchess of Kent's home.

Britain was taking no chances. Parliament asked the Duke of Wellington to call up the military. Wellington had led the British forces that defeated Napoleon at the Battle of Waterloo in 1815. Protesters were no match for him. Soon, cavalrymen armed with lances and the elite infantrymen known as Grenadier Guards waited for orders. Police officers formed a human barrier around Buckingham Palace. Thousands of deputy constables also stood ready to defend the city. The confrontation would end "to the credit of the Government and the country," predicted the seventy-nine-year-old duke.

On the day of the protest, Londoners woke up to a steady rain. Thousands of people who had said they would march stayed home. Still, twenty thousand or more demonstrators showed up at the starting place, Kennington Common, across the river Thames from the heart of the city. They would have marched, if only the Duke of Wellington had not secured all the bridges crossing the Thames, and if only their shoes were not sinking in mud. When the police offered to escort a Chartist leader to the House of Commons, he accepted. The petition he delivered bore close to two million signatures—a great number, but far fewer than the Chartists had promised. Many were forged, among them those of the Duke of Wellington and Queen Victoria. Others were made-up names: "No Cheese," "Pugnose," "Mr. Punch." The lawmakers could hardly take such a petition seriously.

Despite fears of a violent clash, April 10 was a peaceful day in London. The date marked the high point of the Chartist movement. Followers began drifting away, and Chartism died out. Not until 1918 would all British men over twenty-one gain the right to vote. Women would be granted equal voting rights with men in 1928.

"I never was calmer and quieter, or less nervous," Queen Victoria boasted when the protest was over. "Great events make me calm; it is only trifles that irritate my nerves." Perhaps she was telling the truth and had not been frightened by the demonstration, but it had made her angry. Most British workers were loyal to their

April 10, 1848: followers of the Chartist movement gather on Kennington Common.

nation and their queen, she believed. The protest, she declared, had been led by "wanton & worthless men" who were out to weaken the nation by pitting one economic class against another.

Yet thousands of her subjects were suffering from want, including many children. To help support their families, youngsters were employed illegally in coal mines and as chimney sweeps. Although it was against the law for factories to employ children younger than nine, many boys and girls age six and younger were being sent to work. The law stated that factory children could work no more than ten hours a day, but child laborers commonly put in longer workdays. They did boring, repetitive tasks. They were exposed to toxic chemicals, and operated dangerous machinery. "They seldom lose the hand," said one callous proprietor about the children running a punching machine in his nail factory. "It only takes off a finger at the first or second joint." When this happened, he added, the fault was the child's "sheer carelessness." For all the drudgery and risk, working children earned a pittance. They wore rags and often had no shoes. They had no time for school or outdoor play.

Across the Irish Sea, a terrible famine had claimed a million lives and forced another million Irish to emigrate. For several years in a row, a blight had destroyed the potato crop that fed much of the population. Ireland had been part of Great Britain since 1800, but the government had done shamefully little to ease the people's misery. Some legislators viewed the famine as an economic problem that should be left alone to correct itself. Others in largely Protestant England claimed that God had caused the famine to punish Ireland's many Roman Catholics for their faith.

Victoria came to believe that people of means should help those beneath them. She and Albert set an example by giving generously to charities, including Irish famine relief. Albert also toured a London slum. As a man he could move freely in the world and do things considered improper for a respectable woman, even the queen, to do. Albert saw people gaunt with hunger who were dressed in filthy shreds of

Poor, starving Irish people look with hopelessness at the meager yield from their failed potato crop.

garments. He inspected the crumbling houses where they lived. The experience left the prince feeling appalled and needing to speak out. Victoria helped him write a speech that he delivered at London's Exeter Hall. Albert spoke, he said, on behalf of the population that had "most of the toil, and least of the enjoyments of this world." He urged his affluent listeners to do whatever they could to better conditions for those less fortunate. "To show how man can help man," he said, "ought to be the aim of every philanthropic person; but it is more particularly the duty of those who, under the blessing of Divine Providence, enjoy station, wealth, and education."

As a young queen, Victoria had been schooled by Lord Melbourne to turn away from poverty. Now she was learning a different lesson. She still held Lord Melbourne in high regard, though. She was at Osborne House, helping her children with their own lessons on the evening of November 24, 1848, when word reached

her that Lord Melbourne had died. He had suffered of a stroke at his country home at the age of sixty-nine. "Truly and sincerely do I deplore the loss of one who was a most kind and disinterested friend of mine," Victoria wrote in her journal. "He was indeed, for the first two years of my reign, almost the only friend I had." And so he was. Queen Victoria had millions of subjects, a big family, numerous advisors, and acquaintances in high places, but both before and after Melbourne, she had very few friends.

CHAPTER VII

THE MODERN WORLD

M AY 1, 1851, was no ordinary Thursday. It was opening day for the Great Exhibition, one of the wonders of the nineteenth century.

Drizzle had been falling all morning, but the sky cleared as the royal procession reached its destination. A misty haze rose from the warming grass in London's Hyde Park as Queen Victoria gazed up at a monumental structure gleaming in the sun. People called it the Crystal Palace, and for good reason. It stood sixty-four feet high and nearly two thousand feet long, and it was made of glass. This marvel of engineering housed an enormous display of everything modern or exotic. On view were steam engines like those that powered industry and an electrical telegraph, which could carry messages across a continent at lightning speed. There were fine porcelains from Germany, colorful silks from India, embroideries stitched in Tunisia, and carpets woven in Persia. On show too were the countless manufactured goods that affluent Britons stuffed into their homes, from ornamental clocks to silver tea services, from globes to bronze statuettes. The curious could even stare at a map of the moon.

Onlookers cheer as the queen's party leaves Buckingham Palace, headed for the Great Exhibition.

One of the exhibition's organizers had been Prince Albert. He had seen the project through to completion despite people's fears that the big glass building would come crashing down in the first strong wind. Some pessimists had predicted that the millions of tourists flocking to the Crystal Palace would attract thieves and revolutionaries. They might also cause food shortages or bring bubonic plague into the city. Albert was sure the dire forecasts would be proven wrong, and they were.

On opening day, the queen and prince brought their two oldest children. With

Albert escorting Vicky, who was ten, and Victoria holding nine-year-old Bertie by the hand, the four stepped inside to roaring cheers. Drums rolled and trumpets blared, loud and jubilant. Victoria was dressed gaudily, in a pink and silver dress and a headdress of diamonds and feathers. She sat on a raised throne before a fountain and listened as Albert told the twenty-five thousand spectators that the Crystal Palace had been completed in seven months. He reported with pride that it showcased the products of Great Britain, its colonies, and countries through-out the world. He praised the cooperation among nations that had made the whole endeavor possible. Next, Victoria expressed her hope that the exhibition would ben-efit humanity "by encouraging the arts of peace and industry, strengthening the bonds of union among the nations of the earth, and promoting a friendly and hon-ourable rivalry."

Everyone then spread out to explore the building's galleries. The queen was fascinated by the machinery on exhibit, including a printing press that could turn out ten thousand pages an hour and an alarm bed that tossed a sleeper onto the floor. "The exhibition," she wrote, "has taught me so much I never knew before—has brought me into contact with so many clever people I should never have known otherwise." Reflecting on the whole experience, she called it "one of the greatest and most glorious days of our lives, with which, to my pride and joy, the name of my dearly beloved Albert is for ever associated!" She would return to the Crystal Palace many times before October 11, when it closed.

Opening day had begun with a breakfast celebration for Prince Arthur, who was turning a year old. Arthur had been born with a sunny disposition. He was kind by nature and quickly became his mother's favorite child. "It gives me a pang if any fault is found in his looks and character," Victoria said about Arthur, "and the bare thought of his growing out of my hands and being exposed to danger—makes the tears come to my eyes."

Child number eight, Prince Leopold, entered the world in April 1853. His

Amid palm trees, fountains, and statues in the Crystal Palace, Prince Albert delivers his opening address. The queen and her two oldest children stand on a raised platform and listen.

parents would soon learn that he had hemophilia, a rare inherited disorder that leaves the blood unable to clot. At the time no treatment had been found, so every injury posed a risk of uncontrolled bleeding. Most babies born with hemophilia died in childhood.

Worry about the infant coupled with postpartum depression—what Victoria called her "lowness and tendency to cry"—made her harder to get along with than

ever. She raged at Albert over trifles, forcing him to retreat to a quiet place. Once she stormed about for an hour because he mentioned that she had turned to the wrong page in a book. Afraid to approach his wife in person, Albert wrote, "I am often astonished at the effect which a hasty word of mine has produced."

At Osborne, at least, Victoria found peace. She and Albert liked their island home so much that in 1852 they bought a second retreat, in Scotland. Balmoral Castle was farther from London than Osborne House. Surrounded by forests, hills, and crags, it was "a pretty little castle in the old Scottish style," Victoria wrote. Balmoral pleased the eye, but like the original Osborne House, it was too small. It lacked sitting rooms, so government ministers conducted business with the queen while she sat on her bed. Everyone crowded into the billiard room after dinner. Ladies had to rise from their chairs and move away from the billiard table to avoid being struck by a gentleman's cue.

As he did at Osborne, Albert designed a new structure and had the old one torn down. He borrowed ideas from castles he had seen in Germany and Belgium and throughout Scotland. To Victoria the result—"my dearest Albert's *own* creation"—was beautiful. "His great taste, and the impress of his dear hand, have been stamped everywhere," she said. The new Balmoral Castle had big windows to let in sunlight. They offered stunning views of the river Dee and the rolling, wooded hills beyond it.

Victoria loved everything about life at Balmoral. She hiked or rode on horseback to picturesque spots such as Garmaddie Wood or Creag a' Mhortair (Rock of the Murderer). Whatever grisly story gave rise to that name was long forgotten. "All seemed to breathe freedom and peace," she said. She continually praised the Scottish country folk, the scenery, and the streams that were as "clear as glass." Even the grass in Scotland was "delightfully soft to walk upon," she remarked. Lady Lyttelton mocked the queen's exuberance in a letter to her daughter: "Scotch air, Scotch people, Scotch hills, Scotch rivers, Scotch woods, are all far preferable to those of any other nation in or out of this world."

Creating a *tableau vivant*, or "living picture," was a form of entertainment in the Victorian period. The costumed participants remained silent and completely still as an audience gazed on the scene they created. The royal children presented this tableau of the four seasons for their parents' wedding anniversary. From left to right: Alice as spring, Arthur and Vicky as summer, Helena as the spirit empress, Alfred as autumn, and Louise and Bertie as winter.

The queen and prince consort chose Scottish plaids for Balmoral's curtains, wallpaper, carpets, and upholstery. Any spot not covered in a tartan was adorned with thistles, the centuries-old symbol of Scotland. Before long, Victoria started speaking with a Scottish brogue whenever she stayed at Balmoral. Albert and the young princes wore kilts. The family ate Scottish breakfasts of oatmeal and smoked haddock, and bagpipers entertained during dinner.

And guests hated the place. Lord Rosebery, a member of Parliament, thought Balmoral had the ugliest drawing room in the world. Lord Clarendon, a British diplomat, was one of many people who complained that the castle was too cold. His toes grew numb during dinner—surely, he grumbled, he was in danger of frostbite! The queen liked bracing temperatures and kept the windows open on all but the most frigid days. When fires were allowed, they were too small to radiate any warmth. Another statesman, Lord Salisbury, obtained an order from his doctor to have his room heated to a comfortable temperature. The queen's ministers also objected to the long journey they had to make from London to Balmoral and back again. New railroads connected these distant parts of Britain, but the trip still took two days. The ministers asked, ever so politely, if Her Majesty would please spend less time in Scotland, but she dismissed their requests.

Albert contentedly fished and stalked deer in the wild country around the castle. Once in a while, he let Bertie join him on these jaunts. Victoria and Albert worried about their oldest son. Bertie was a normal, average child, but his parents wanted him to be better than the best. They expected more from someone likely to be king of Great Britain, and they were determined to make him smarter. They were also going to ensure that he had strong morals so he would be nothing like Victoria's royal uncles, who had chased women and sired sons and daughters outside of marriage.

While the other children learned from governesses, Bertie studied with a tutor. In 1849, his parents hired a young teacher named Henry Birch to see that the

Balmoral Castle in its beautiful setting, surrounded by forests and mountains.

seven-year-old Prince of Wales mastered a broad range of subjects. Bertie was under orders to work at everything from reading and writing to memorizing and reciting, drawing and music, German, French, and arithmetic. Victoria and Albert gave Birch instructions: Bertie was to study six days a week. He would be allowed to see his brothers and sisters only on Sundays, and he was to be kept away from other boys his age, who might be a bad influence.

Bertie reacted as many healthy, spirited children would, by throwing temper tantrums. Some days he yelled and cried so much that he wore himself out. After three months on the job, Birch tried to tell the boy's parents that outdoor exercise might benefit Bertie more than constant studying. He also assured the queen and prince that his pupil was making progress. "There are few English boys who know so much French or German or know so much general information," he reported, but Victoria and Albert demanded more. Whatever Bertie did was never good enough.

It took a year for Bertie to understand that Birch was on his side. "I seem to have got at his heart, and he seems to have given up the struggle against authority," Birch noted with relief. So in January 1852, when Henry Birch left his job to become a priest in the Church of England, the ten-year-old felt heartbroken. He looked for ways to show his love for the tutor who had been his friend. "It has been a terrible sorrow to the Prince of Wales, who has done no end of touching things since he heard that he was to lose him," wrote Lady Canning, who liked and understood Bertie. "He is such an affectionate, dear little boy; his little notes and presents, which Mr. Birch used to find on his pillow, were really too moving."

Bertie's new tutor was a well-educated lawyer, Frederick Waymouth Gibbs. Gibbs was young—just twenty-nine—but he was already set in his ways. He was

The queen and prince consort had the rooms at
Balmoral decorated in Scottish plaids and thistles.

a somber, critical man, just the type to follow the new, even harsher rules that the queen and Prince Albert put in place. Bertie now had lessons seven days a week, from eight in the morning until six at night. Other tutors came to the palace to train the young prince in riding, dancing, and military drills. The royal parents wanted their son to fall into bed each night too exhausted to give anyone trouble.

Bertie hated the new tutor and did everything he could to make Gibbs's life miserable. He spat, sneered, threw things across the room, and used vulgar language. Hearing reports of Bertie's stubbornness, Baron Stockmar remembered a willful little girl he had known decades before. The Prince of Wales was "an exaggerated Copy of his Mother," he concluded.

As Bertie rebelled and everyone coped with Queen Victoria's unstable moods, war broke out in a distant part of the world. The dispute that triggered the conflict was over control of the Church of the Nativity, an ancient site in Bethlehem that Christians held sacred. Bethlehem lay within Turkey's Ottoman Empire, which encompassed much of the land bordering the Mediterranean and Black Seas. Turkey had agreed to let France, a Roman Catholic country, have authority over the church, but Russia, a largely Orthodox Christian nation, objected. The issue divided the many Christian pilgrims in Bethlehem, and in the summer of 1853, they rioted. When violence claimed the lives of several Orthodox monks, Russia blamed Turkish police for failing to protect them. A Russian army marched south. British leaders worried that the Russians might sweep into Turkey and seize control of the straits that linked the Black and Mediterranean Seas. If that happened, Britain could lose access to an important trade route to its eastern colonies.

On November 30, a Russian naval fleet attacked and sank a Turkish flotilla in the Black Sea. Russian sailors then picked up rifles and shot at the survivors struggling to stay afloat. The deaths of four thousand Turks in the massacre outraged many Britons. The current prime minister, Lord Aberdeen, was a man of peace, but the sharp-minded home secretary, Lord Palmerston, wanted to stop Russia at all costs. Public opinion was on Palmerston's side. Parliament debated, and on March

28, 1854, Great Britain declared war on Russia, just as France had done the day before. The opposing armies fought some of their fiercest, most devastating battles on the Crimean Peninsula, which juts into the northern Black Sea. History would remember this conflict as the Crimean War.

Queen Victoria did all she could to support her nation's fighting men. She felt close to them because she herself was a soldier's daughter, although she had no memories of her father, the Duke of Kent. She studied maps and followed the movements of her "beloved troops" from afar. "You never saw anyone so taken up with military affairs as she is," said Lord Panmure, the minister for war. She reviewed troops; she knitted socks, scarves, and mittens for the soldiers on the front lines; and she wrote condolence letters to widows of men killed in battle.

Accompanied by their sons, Victoria and Albert inspect soldiers who have returned from the Crimean War.

Having enjoyed peace for nearly forty years, Britain's army was unprepared for war. Most of its gentleman officers were too young to have seen combat. Even the older ones had never led troops on active service. As journalists telegraphed reports from the Crimean region, Britons read in their newspapers about battles lost and men dying far from home, often needlessly. They read, for example, how an officer had mistakenly sent a cavalry unit on a disastrous charge into a valley lined with Russian guns. Of the 670 men who rode into the valley, 118 were killed and 127 were wounded.

Making a bad situation worse, the army had a bungling bureaucratic system for getting supplies to the front lines. Soldiers in winter camps went without warm coats and blankets. The sick and wounded men who filled the army's hellish hospitals in the war zone slept on dirty floors. They wore filthy clothing, ate rancid food, and died in large numbers. A desperate government called upon a woman, the nurse Florence Nightingale, to bring order, cleanliness, and healing to the faraway hospitals.

Public outrage at the handling of the war led to a wintry riot in London's Trafalgar Square. Protesters threw snowballs at horse-drawn buses and cabs, at pedestrians, and at the police who came to restore order. More significantly, public opinion brought about a change in leadership. Lord Aberdeen stepped down as prime minister, and the shrewd Lord Palmerston took on the role.

Victoria wanted to do more. She wished she could travel to the scenes of war and accomplish something important, as Florence Nightingale was doing. "I envy her for being able to do so much good & look after those noble brave heroes whose behaviour is so admirable," she wrote.

On March 5, 1855, accompanied by Albert and her two oldest children, the queen journeyed by train to the southern county of Kent to visit convalescing soldiers who were back from the war zone. While being escorted through wards at the Fort Pitt Army Hospital, Victoria handed out medals and spoke with each man who was confined to bed. She saw ghastly injuries. An exploding artillery shell had

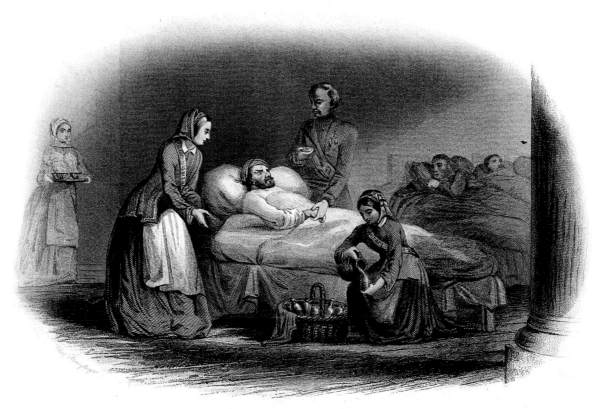

Queen Victoria admired Florence Nightingale, the pioneering woman who oversaw nursing in the military hospitals in Turkey. Here Nightingale and her nurses tend to an ailing soldier.

taken away thirteen pieces of one man's skull; another soldier, a cavalryman, had had his leg crushed when his horse was shot and fell on him. Upon hearing kind words from their sovereign, many of the men broke down and wept.

Victoria, too, looked ready to cry at the sight of "such fine, powerful frames laid low and prostrate with wounds and sickness on beds of suffering," as she wrote. But she forced back her tears and completed her rounds. When the patients at a second hospital, at Brompton, called out, "God bless our Queen," it was too much for her to bear, and she began sobbing. She canceled a speech she had planned to give; she was too distraught to face an audience, having seen just a small part of the ugliness of war.

France's ruler also wanted to play a larger role. In 1852, Louis Napoleon had declared himself emperor of France and was now known as Napoleon III. He had recently announced his intention to go to the Crimean Peninsula and take command of the French and British armies. Military leaders wanted to stop him, knowing

he would only be in the way. Understanding that the situation had to be handled delicately, the prime minister, Lord Palmerston, came up with a way to resolve it. He enlisted Queen Victoria to carry out a diplomatic mission and persuade the emperor to change his mind. So without mentioning the reason, the queen and her government invited Napoleon III and his wife, Empress Eugénie, to Windsor Castle for a state visit.

On April 16, 1855, Victoria waited nervously for her guests. Only when Napoleon III greeted her in the French way, with a kiss on either cheek, did she feel at ease. Like his uncle Napoleon I, the current emperor was a short man. He had waxed his long mustache and twisted it into two sharp points. Victoria liked his face and his calm dignity. Upon getting to know him, she decided he was "possessed of *indomitable courage, unflinching firmness of purpose, self-reliance, perseverance and great*

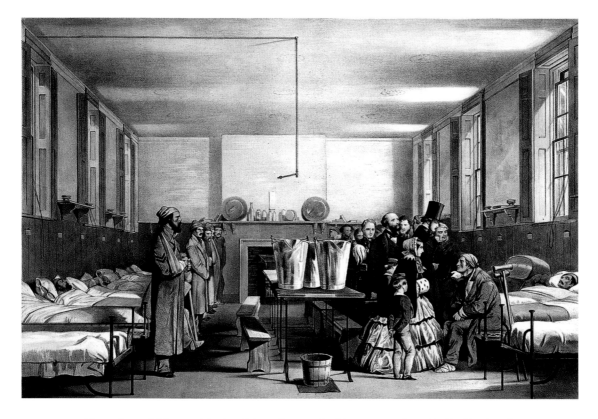

Victoria and Albert visit the sick and wounded in an army hospital in England.

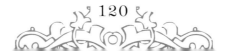

Left: Impatient with the slow progress in the Crimean region, Napoleon III threatened to go to the theater of war and take command. **Right:** The congenial Empress Eugénie was a model of style and sophistication.

secrecy." The beautiful Empress Eugénie captivated both Victoria and Albert. She was a "charming lovable creature," in Victoria's opinion, "lively & talkative."

A state visit was always meticulously planned. The national leaders were kept busy attending formal dinners, balls, and concerts, and reviewing military units. Nevertheless, the British queen and French emperor found time to talk. Napoleon III told Victoria that he had been born under a lucky star, that an unseen force controlled his destiny. Now it was leading him to the scene of battle. The generals there were weak, but he would stir them into action. Victoria reminded him that the Crimean Peninsula was a long way from France. War zones were dangerous places, she said. Napoleon III waved off the queen's concerns, but she managed to get through to him. He never went to the front lines.

CHAPTER VIII

"Oh, This Is Death"

NAPOLEON III and Eugénie insisted on repaying the hospitality shown to them by the British royal couple. For this reason, Victoria and Albert made a state visit to Paris in August 1855, while the Crimean War was still being fought. Vicky and Bertie accompanied them.

The emperor and empress escorted their guests to the opera and theater. They brought the British royals to see such famous sights as Notre Dame Cathedral and the Louvre, the historic palace turned art museum. The sweltering summer heat caused a member of Napoleon III's retinue to remark that he would trade all the great works in the Louvre, even the famed statue Venus de Milo, for a single glass of lemonade. Victoria, the queen who kept her castles cold, appeared not to mind the stifling temperatures. She announced that elegant, bejeweled Paris was the most beautiful city she had ever seen—although in truth she had seen very few.

As had happened in Brussels twelve years before, people noticed the queen's odd clothes. On one occasion, "she had on a massive bonnet of white silk with streamers behind and a tuft of maribou feathers on top," observed General Canrobert of

the French army. "She had a mantle and a sunshade of crude green which did not seem to go with the rest of her costume." Worst of all, Canrobert thought, was the enormous pocketbook Queen Victoria carried on her arm. It was "like those of our grandmothers—made of white satin or silk, on which was embroidered a fat poodle in gold." No criticism reached the queen's ears. Instead, people were careful to compliment her. "I was thought so dignified . . . and was so well-dressed (which considering all the trouble I took I am glad to hear)," she concluded.

Princess Vicky truly was elegantly clothed, thanks to her hostess's foresight. While in England the chic Empress Eugénie had observed the queen's frumpy wardrobe. After going home she sent the princess royal some dresses as a gift, so the girl would feel fashionable when she came to Paris.

No one had a better time on this trip than Bertie, though. He found everything in Paris to be wondrous: the throngs of beautiful people on the boulevards, the fireworks exploding over the Palace of Versailles, the scrumptious meals that he was served. Believing he could have a happier life in Paris than at home, Bertie told Napoleon III, "I should like to be your son."

The Crimean War ended in February 1856, and on March 30, the warring parties signed a treaty in Paris. No nation could claim victory, and they all had to reckon with great loss of life. More than twenty-one thousand British soldiers had died, most of them from disease. At the time of the treaty, Britain was fighting another, briefer war. It was defending the ancient city of Herat, which is now part of Afghanistan, from an invasion by Persia (present-day Iran). Herat had declared its independence and placed itself under the protection of the British in India. That war ended in a victory for Britain on April 4, 1857.

Ten days later, on April 14, Queen Victoria gave birth to her ninth child, Princess Beatrice. Her oldest, Princess Victoria, was already sixteen and engaged to marry Prince Frederick Wilhelm of Prussia. How quickly time sped away!

The French emperor and empress welcome their guests from England.

HER MAJESTY, PRINCE ALBERT AND THE ROYAL FAMILY.

This popular print depicts Queen Victoria, Prince Albert, and their nine children.

Frederick had proposed while visiting Balmoral with his parents, and Queen Victoria was thrilled. She was grateful to God, she wrote, "for *one* of the happiest days of my life!" "Fritz," she thought, was such a handsome, sincere, good-natured man. Prince Albert favored the match for political reasons. He foresaw that Prussia and the other German states would one day come together as a unified nation, and he wanted the bond between Britain and that new Germany to be strong.

The queen kept a watchful eye on the courting couple, perhaps recalling all the kissing that went on during her own engagement. Vicky and Fritz were forbidden

to be alone in a room unless the door was open and Vicky's strict mother sat in the next chamber. National interests had brought the pair together, but anyone could see that Vicky and Fritz were fond of each other. Victoria, as mother and queen, made sure they behaved properly.

The wedding took place on January 25, 1858, in the Chapel Royal at St. James's Palace, where the queen and Prince Albert had been united eighteen years before. "I felt as if I were being married over again myself, only much more nervous," Queen Victoria said. She feared that she might fall to pieces as she watched her "darling flower" walk down the aisle between Prince Albert and King Leopold. Yet she held herself together through the ceremony and the wedding breakfast the next day. Not until Vicky and her prince departed for Prussia, where they were to live, did Victoria break down and cry. She suddenly felt "so lost without Vicky," she said. No longer was her firstborn "an innocent girl," Victoria knew, "but a wife—&—*perhaps, this* time *next year* already a mother!" If Vicky returned to England, it would be "but for a short time, almost as a visitor!" Desperate to feel close to her faraway daughter, the queen sent long letters to Vicky at least twice a week.

Victoria added this correspondence to the vast amount of paperwork that demanded her attention. Stacks of documents reached her desk every day, each one requiring her signature or comment. Countless letters from government officials, military commanders, and foreign leaders awaited her reply. She and Albert worked as a team. He drafted the responses, and she copied them. Albert, whose first language was German, depended on Victoria to correct his English. Also, Victoria's correspondents expected to receive letters written by the queen's hand.

Many of the papers that reached Victoria in 1858 had to do with India. Britain held dominion over immense stretches of India, which provided raw materials for British industry, especially cotton for weaving cloth, indigo for dyeing it, and opium for making medicines. Parliament and the queen ruled the colony through the East India Company, an old and powerful trading firm. The British living in India set themselves apart from the people and culture that surrounded them.

Queen Victoria was so nervous on Vicky's wedding day that she could not hold still for the several seconds required to take a photograph in 1858. As a result her image is blurred.

They socialized with one another at dinner parties, receptions, balls, and tennis matches, much as they would have done in England. They lived in big houses with broad verandas and had staffs of Indian servants to wait on them.

The East India Company had formed armies of Indian soldiers, who were known as sepoys, to protect British holdings. In the 1850s, army leaders supplied the Indian forces with new rifles and paper-wrapped cartridges that held gunpowder and bullets. To load his weapon, a soldier pulled open the cartridge with his teeth and rammed its contents into the rifle barrel. To keep moisture out, the cartridges were coated at the factory with grease, sometimes with the fat of cattle or pigs. This was a small matter to the British, but not to the Indians in their armies. Most were Hindus, who held cows sacred and never ate beef. Others were Muslims and therefore were forbidden to eat pork. By expecting the men to put these cartridges to their lips, the British were asking them to go against religious teachings.

The British understood their error in early 1857 and canceled orders for the offensive cartridges, but it was too late to stop distrust from spreading. On April 23, in the military encampment at Meerut, India, eighty-five men in a cavalry regiment refused to handle cartridges they feared had been tainted. The men were court-martialed and sentenced to long prison terms. On May 9, the British shamed them further by forcing them to march in chains past all the soldiers garrisoned at Meerut.

The next day, the sepoys of Meerut revolted. They freed the prisoners, killed British officers and their families, and burned their houses. They then moved on to Delhi, fifty miles away, where they continued to kill. The mutiny spread across northern India to the Ganges River port of Cawnpore (now Kanpur), where, on June 26, Indian soldiers and civilians shot at hundreds of Britons trying to leave by boat. The Indians captured some two hundred women and children; on July 17, they hacked these prisoners to death and threw their remains down a well.

A devastated Queen Victoria read newspaper reports of "the horrors committed

The British called the Indians serving in their armed forces sepoys. The term *sepoy* derives from the Persian word *sepāhī*, meaning "soldier."

in India on poor ladies & children," as she wrote. She thought about the murders "*day* and night." It was dreadful for such things to happen anywhere, but especially in beautiful India, the colony she called the jewel in her crown.

The queen felt for the British people who had died, but Britain was equally guilty of cruelty in India. British forces had responded to the mutiny by killing hundreds of innocent Indians. They tied some captured mutineers to the mouths of cannons and blew their bodies to bits. They forced others to lick the blood of

murdered women and children from the walls of Cawnpore—whether these prisoners had taken part in the massacre hardly mattered.

Victoria was appalled; she pleaded for justice and kindness. The people of India needed to know, she said, "that there is no hatred to a brown skin—none." She wrote a proclamation that was read aloud at every Indian military post on November 1, 1858. It announced that the East India Company had been abolished. From that day forward, the queen and her government would rule India directly. Through the proclamation Victoria pardoned all mutineers not guilty of murder. She wanted to spread "feelings of generosity, benevolence and religious toleration" and "draw a veil over the sad and bloody past." Britain soon regained control of the places in rebellion, but many in government remained wary. Was the uprising a onetime occurrence, or did it foreshadow an Indian fight for independence? It was impossible to know.

Albert had helped the proclamation. He was working hard—too hard. He was weighed down by concerns abroad and at home. If he was not anxious about the condition of the poor, then he was pondering the massacre in India, the readiness of the British military, the Crimean War, or another war that was being fought between Austria and France. His stomach was chronically upset, and his teeth gave him pain. He was always cold and had taken to wearing a wig to keep his head warm. He was filled with gloom and dread. One day at Osborne, while planting some saplings, he said to Victoria, "I shall never see them grow up." Victoria told him not to be silly. He was far too young for such melancholy thoughts. But he insisted that he would die before the trees matured.

Once, Albert had longed for work and even thrived on it. Now work was getting the better of him, and he needed a holiday. In September 1860 he and Victoria left England for a restful stay in Coburg, Germany, his childhood home. By a sad coincidence, Albert's stepmother died while they were traveling, and they arrived just in time to attend her funeral. Loved ones dressed in black mourning clothes waited

to greet them. Baron Stockmar and Albert's brother Ernst were there to offer words of condolence. Vicky had come with her eighteen-month-old son, Wilhelm. "Such a little love!" Victoria exclaimed about her grandson. "He has Fritz's eyes and Vicky's mouth and very curly hair. . . . We felt so happy to see him at last." Wilhelm had a sister, who had been left with her nurses in Prussia. Her name was Charlotte, and she was just two months old.

One day, Albert left his wife and daughter sketching outdoors and went for a carriage ride in the countryside. Suddenly his horses bolted. Seeing that his conveyance was headed for a crash, Albert threw himself to the ground. He suffered only scrapes and bruises, but the accident left him scared and shaken. (One horse died in in the mishap; the others ran back to Coburg, where they were caught.) Not long afterward, on his last day in his hometown, Albert went for a walk with Ernst. When they reached a scenic spot, Albert took a handkerchief from his pocket and wiped his face. At first Ernst thought one of Albert's wounds from the accident had started bleeding again. Instead, "tears were trickling down his cheeks," Ernst said. They were tears of farewell to a place Albert had loved. "He persisted in declaring that he was well aware that he had been here for the last time in his life."

Albert's sense that death was approaching proved true, but it didn't come for him. On March 16, 1861, the Duchess of Kent died of cancer, at seventy-four. Victoria, comprehending that her mother was dead, collapsed in grief. "It is *dreadful, dreadful* to think we shall never see that dear kind loving face again," she lamented. One crying fit followed another. "*She* is gone! That *precious, dearly beloved tender* Mother . . . without whom I can't *imagine life.*" Albert tried to comfort his wife, but she would not be consoled. "I do not wish to feel better," she confessed to Vicky. The queen's sorrow was sharpened by regret. As an adult she had kept her mother at a distance, focusing on past wrongs. Now, as she sorted through the duchess's treasured possessions, she saw her mistake. She wrote to Vicky, "Such touching relics I have found! Her love for me is beyond everything! Not a scrap of my writing—or

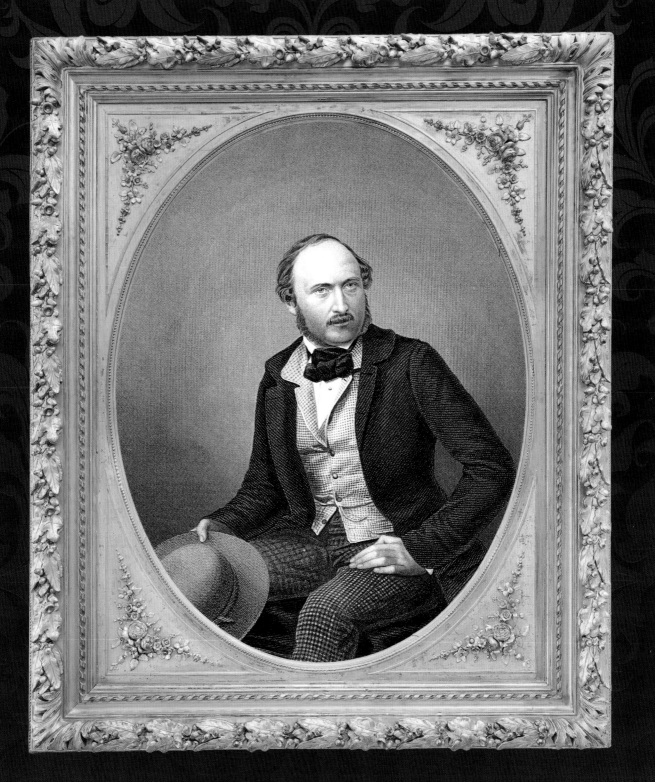

Prince Albert had premonitions of death.

of my hair has ever been thrown away—and such touching notes in a book about my babyhood." Too late the queen understood how deeply and faithfully her mother had loved her.

Victoria ate alone; twice a day she went to the gardens at Frogmore, adjoining Windsor Castle, where her mother was buried, "as if it was a satisfaction to feed her grief," the diplomat Lord Clarendon told a friend. "She never ceases crying." The already overtaxed Albert added Victoria's workload to his own.

Concern about her children pulled Victoria's attention away from the past and into the present. Eight-year-old Leopold was pale and weak and prone to bruising due to his hemophilia. His doctors wanted him to spend the winter in a warm place, where he could build up his strength outdoors. Victoria and Albert arranged for Leopold to go to southern France in the care of Sir Edward Bowater, an aging army veteran whom the boy liked. Lady Bowater and the Bowaters' nineteen-year-old daughter, Louisa, would be wintering in France as well. "[Leopold] cried when I kissed him—and wished him good-bye," Queen Victoria wrote to Vicky, "but he was in good spirits otherwise."

Victoria also despaired over Bertie. For a time she and Albert had been pleased with their oldest son. He had made good progress in his studies, and in 1860 he had represented the royal family on a tour of North America. Nineteen-year-old Bertie's excellent French had endeared him to many Canadians. His friendly, congenial manner had made him popular in St. Louis, Chicago, and Washington, D.C. New Yorkers had come out to cheer him when he paraded along Broadway. Then, in 1861, he went to an Irish army encampment for military training.

While in Ireland, Bertie formed an intimate relationship with an Irish actress named Nellie Clifden, who had slept with other soldiers. He continued to see her after he returned to England to further his studies at Trinity College in Cambridge. Because he was a high-ranking member of the royal family, news of his activities got around. London gentlemen began discussing the Prince of Wales and his love life

when they gathered at their clubs. Before long, the stories reached Prince Albert, who repeated them to the queen.

For Bertie this romance was a passing attachment, part of growing up and exploring adult life. His parents reacted to it, though, as if he had done a terrible thing. It seemed to them that despite their efforts to force Bertie onto the right path in life, he was headed in the wrong direction. Picturing him with mistresses and illegitimate offspring, Victoria was horrified. Was Nellie Clifden imagining herself as the Princess of Wales? Suppose she became pregnant! Victoria wrote in her journal that she would never again look at her son without a shudder.

Recalling the shameful behavior of Victoria's royal uncles, Bertie's parents worried about his moral character.

There was but one solution, the queen and prince consort decided. Bertie must marry, and the sooner the better. They even picked out a suitable bride. Princess Alexandra, the oldest daughter of Prince Christian of Denmark, was still in her teens. She was a devout churchgoer and skilled with a needle and thread. "It would be a thousand pities if you were to lose her," Prince Albert advised the heir to the throne.

On November 25, despite having a cold, Albert made a hasty trip to Cambridge. He and Bertie discussed the young prince's future during a long walk in the rain. Bertie had met Princess Alexandra; he had called her "charming and very pretty." But he insisted that he was not yet ready to take a wife. Albert woke up the next

morning to find that his cold had worsened. He had a pounding head and pains in his arms and legs. He returned to London believing he had failed.

Albert's health deteriorated. He ate little, slept poorly, and spent days in his dressing gown. Dr. James Clark told Victoria that she had no reason to worry, but she worried anyway. When a sleepless Albert wandered from room to room at night, Victoria followed him in tears. He moved into Windsor Castle's sunny Blue Room— the same room where King George IV and King William IV had died.

A team of doctors now attended to the prince. One, named Dr. Watson, assured Queen Victoria that he had successfully treated "many infinitely worse cases." Dr. Watson was more honest with the prime minister, however, informing him, "The malady is very grave and serious."

Victoria entered the Blue Room on the bleak, cloudy morning of December 13 to find her husband lying in bed and gasping for every breath. Albert's lungs were filling with fluid. "I prayed & cried as if I should go mad," Victoria stated later, "for he was my Life!" Capable Princess Alice had a message telegraphed to the Prince of Wales at college, summoning him home. Bertie arrived full of good cheer, but he turned quiet and somber as soon as he saw his father.

On the night of December 14, the most dreaded of visitors dropped in on the royal family again. Victoria was at Albert's bedside, holding his hand, when she sensed a change come over him. "Oh, this is death," she suddenly said. Albert took one gentle breath, a second, and a third, and then he breathed no more. Victoria rose and kissed the forehead of her cherished partner in life. "Oh my dear Darling!" she cried, and she collapsed to her knees. Albert had died young, at age forty-two.

Vicky and Leopold received telegrams bringing news of their father's death. It was a doubly dismal day for young Leopold, because Sir Edward Bowater, the man looking after him, had also died on December 14, following a stroke. Lady Bowater and Louisa chose not to accompany Sir Edward's body to England, but to stay in France with Leopold. The prince's "pretty, winning ways greatly endeared him to us both," Louisa Bowater noted, and they could not bear to leave him.

A grieving Leopold longed to be with his mother, but the queen was too caught up in her own sorrow to think of her children's pain. "Poor Mama is more wretched, more miserable—than any being in this World *can* be," Victoria wrote to her sad little son in France. "I pine & long for your dearly beloved precious Papa so dreadfully!"

Following pages: An artist envisioned Albert's last moments in the Blue Room. Among those present are the queen and most of the couple's children; Albert's brother, Ernst; his valet; four doctors; a clergyman; and several statesmen. Albert's doctors listed typhoid fever as his cause of death, but modern medical historians who have studied his symptoms think he died of stomach cancer. Crohn's disease, a chronic inflammatory bowel disorder, has also been suggested as the cause of Albert's death.

CHAPTER IX

WHERE IS QUEEN VICTORIA?

AT MIDNIGHT in quiet London, the bells of St. Paul's Cathedral tolled long and low. As telegraph wires carried news of Prince Albert's death to every part of the nation, church bells in other cities and towns chimed their own dirges.

People in Britain and overseas shared the queen's sorrow. The famed nurse Florence Nightingale praised the prince consort, stating, "What he has done for our country no one knows." Said Sir Moses Montefiore, a leader in London's Jewish community, "We have lost a great and good prince," one who was "most liberal as regards religious freedom to all." A messenger came from France bearing a letter of condolence from Napoleon III and Empress Eugénie.

The humor magazine *Punch* turned serious for a day and published a poetic tribute to Albert. "Him whom she loved we loved," the anonymous poet wrote. "We shared her joy, / And we will not be denied to share her grief."

In Queen Victoria's Britain, etiquette determined what mourners wore and how they behaved. A man might wear dark clothes and a black armband to signify that he was grieving, but a woman dressed all in black. Her only jewelry was made

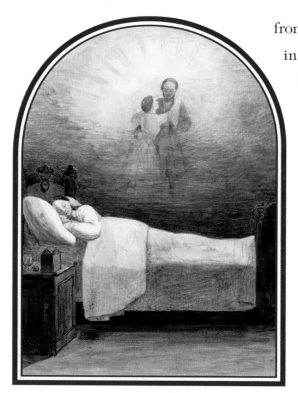

Princess Louise, a talented artist, painted Queen Victoria dreaming of a heavenly reunion with Prince Albert.

from jet, a black semiprecious stone. Those in mourning retreated from society. They avoided the theater and other public places where people had fun. How long someone mourned depended on his or her relation to the deceased. A person who lost a husband or wife mourned for two years. The mourning period was shorter for the deaths of other family members—perhaps a year, six months, or several weeks. As this time neared its end, a woman might add gray, mauve, or touches of white to her wardrobe. She might start wearing jewelry containing a lock of the deceased loved one's hair.

Queen Victoria mourned like no one else. She declared that for the next year, everyone coming to the palace had to dress in black. For as long as she wore deepest mourning, her ladies in waiting had to as well. Throughout Britain, she decreed, "it is expected that all persons do forthwith put themselves into decent mourning." Great Britain became a nation dressed in black.

She took advantage of photography, a new medium, to have pictures made of the Blue Room. They would help the staff at Windsor Castle keep the bedchamber looking as it did on the day Albert died. No detail was too small: the glass from which he had sipped his last medicine was to remain on the bedside table. Every evening, a servant was to lay out Albert's dressing gown and a fresh suit of clothes for the next day, as if he were alive. Victoria covered herself with Albert's coat when

she went to bed at night. She kept a plaster casting of his hand beside her. Unable to face people, Victoria communicated with her Privy Council from an adjoining room. Not even her children could cheer her up. They put on plays, but she sat through the performances glumly.

Victoria had a royal mausoleum built at Frogmore to house Albert's remains. Albert—and, one day, Victoria, too—would lie beneath its high domed ceiling, covered by white marble statues of themselves at rest. Victoria also approved the design for the Albert memorial to be built in London's Kensington Gardens. Topped with a cross, this ornate temple sheltered a gilt-bronze statue of the queen's late husband.

"Oh! how I admired Papa! How in love I was with him! How everything about him was beautiful and precious in my eyes. Oh! how I miss all, all!" she cried out in a letter to Vicky. Victoria thought about killing herself, but, as she confided to her oldest daughter, she decided against it: "A Voice told me for *His* sake—no, 'Still Endure.'"

To Victoria's way of thinking, something—or, more likely, someone—was to blame for Albert's death. She soon singled out that someone: the Prince of Wales. If Bertie had not distressed his father by carrying on with that actress, Victoria was convinced, Albert might still be alive. When Bertie reached out to comfort his mother in her sorrow, she pushed him away. She wanted him out of her sight and out of her thoughts. In February 1862, she sent him on a trip to the far-off Middle East. Bertie was grieving for his father more than Victoria could see. He felt miserable leaving England and believing that she hated him so.

Bertie was home in time for his sister Alice's marriage to Prince Louis of Hesse on July 1, 1862, a dull, windy day. The wedding was a small family affair, befitting a bride who had lost her father six months before. The ceremony was held in the dining room at Osborne House. Prince Albert's brother, Alice's uncle Ernst, had come from Coburg to give away the bride. After making an entrance with her four

Queen Victoria, wearing black as she would for the rest of her life, shows the royal mausoleum to a companion. Prince Albert's remains lie beneath the white statue at the center.

sons, Queen Victoria sat in a corner where a portrait of Albert hung. While Alice and Louis exchanged their vows, she gazed into the eyes of "that blessed guardian angel, that one calm great being that led all."

Victoria still thought that Bertie ought to marry, and at twenty-one he felt ready. He went abroad and proposed to Princess Alexandra of Denmark, and she accepted. The queen insisted, though, that Alexandra's mother be told about her son's romance with Nellie Clifden. She also made sure that thoughts of the deceased Albert overshadowed the engaged couple's happiness. On March 9, 1863, the day before their wedding, she took Bertie and "Alix" to Albert's mausoleum at Frogmore and ushered them inside. "*He* gives you his blessing!" she dramatically proclaimed.

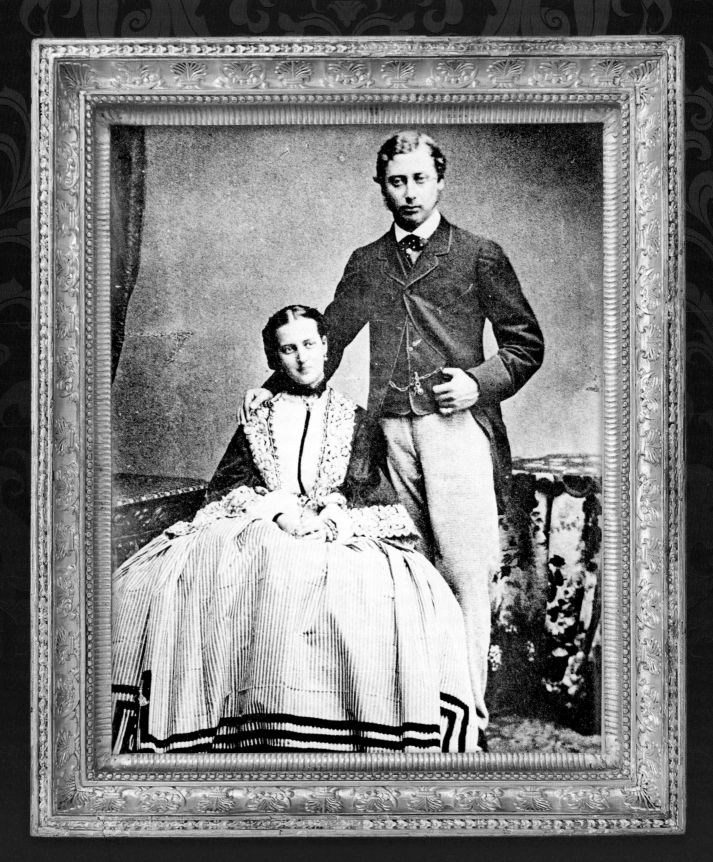

The engaged couple: Princess Alexandra of Denmark and Albert Edward, Prince of Wales.

The queen was duty bound to set aside her grief and tend to the nation, but as 1863 stretched into 1864, her subjects wondered if she ever would. Queen Victoria hid in her royal residences, avoiding the public. Some people asked if their queen was fit to reign, or if Great Britain even needed a monarch. One angry person hung a For Sale sign on the railing outside Buckingham Palace. Victoria maintained that the noise and excitement of going out were more than she could bear, and that no one understood how much she suffered.

Queen Victoria's advisors had a public relations problem on their hands. "Isn't it better to say the Queen can't do so and so because of her health," proposed Dr. William Jenner, who became a royal physician in 1862, "than to say she won't?" A member of Parliament countered that if the queen really was ill, then maybe she should step down and let her son be king. After all, the Prince of Wales was well liked and was often out and about. But 1864 gave way to 1865 with little change.

In February 1866, the queen mustered enough courage to open Parliament. She entered the chamber clothed in black and looked "very stout, very red in the face," according to one unkind witness. "I felt as if I should faint," Victoria said of the ordeal. "All was silent and all eyes fixed upon me, and there I sat alone." The chair that Albert used to occupy stood empty beside her.

On July 5, 1866, Victoria's bashful daughter, Princess Helena, married her German prince, Christian of Schleswig-Holstein, who coughed from smoking and kept a collection of glass eyes. Also in 1866, Prince Arthur, Victoria's favorite son, entered the Royal Military Academy. At sixteen, Arthur was embarking on an army officer's life. Time was forcing Victoria to contend with one change after another: children growing up and moving on, new sons-in-law and a daughter-in-law—and new prime ministers. In 1868 she worked with one of the most memorable, Benjamin Disraeli.

Disraeli was born into a Jewish family, but when he was thirteen his father had him baptized in the Church of England. Church membership opened opportunities

A reluctant Queen Victoria ventured into public to open Parliament in 1866.
She listens as the lord chancellor reads her speech aloud.

for Benjamin, who was to pursue a career in government. Before 1858 the law barred Jews from holding elective office. Unlike most men in Parliament, Disraeli did not grow up in a wealthy home or attend an elite boys' school. By applying his brilliant, witty mind, he had "climbed to the top of the greasy pole" of politics, as he put it, to lead the Conservative Party.

Victoria found Disraeli peculiar, with his rouged cheeks, dyed black ringlets, and corset. She could hardly bear his wife, Mary Anne, who did not know when to be quiet. The queen liked reading the entertaining reports that Disraeli submitted to her, however. And when he praised Prince Albert's manly graces and splendid intellect, he won her loyalty.

Prime Minister Benjamin Disraeli flattered the queen, but he respected her knowledge and experience, and he earned her friendship.

Disraeli had a talent for saying the right thing. "Everyone likes flattery," he said to a friend, "and, when you come to royalty, you should lay it on with a trowel." He told Queen Victoria that her knowledge, experience, and years of working with great men had given her "an advantage in judgement, which few living persons, and probably no living Prince, can rival." Disraeli exaggerated, but Victoria had learned quite a bit about governing during her years as queen.

Less than a year after she settled in to working with Disraeli, Victoria had to get used to another prime minister. Great Britain held a national election in November 1868, and the Liberal Party gained a majority. Heading Her Majesty's government would be William Gladstone, a man Victoria found impossible to like. Gladstone was tall and stern, with the fierce dark eyes of a bird. Disraeli had been warmly devoted, but Gladstone was cold. Disraeli wrote diverting novels in his spare time. Gladstone wrote heavy treatises on ancient Greek poetry. Disraeli had been tactful, but Gladstone could be rude. If the queen voiced her opinion, he would simply say, "Is that so?" Said a frustrated Victoria, "He will not attend to any suggestion but his own mind's."

As a Liberal, Gladstone belonged to the party of Lord Melbourne, but he cared more than Melbourne ever had about the poor and laboring classes. He used his influence as prime minister to get laws passed that improved life for thousands

of Britons. The Education Act of 1870 established locally elected boards to build and manage schools in places where they were needed. The Ballot Act of 1872 let voters elect representatives by marking an *X* on a paper ballot. Before this law was enacted, men declared their votes publicly and they were published for everyone to see. Powerful people used bribes and threats win votes. Other new laws brought safety measures to coal mines, allowed trade unions, and established a national public health system.

Today it is hard to believe that any of these laws caused controversy, but in the 1800s many people questioned the wisdom of educating laborers and their children. They feared that knowledge might make workers unhappy with their lives and cause them to revolt. And politicians who held on to offices through rigged elections resented giving up control. Queen Victoria believed the monarchy, aristocracy, and Church of England were the forces that held society together. She thought Gladstone's measures were weakening Britain's way of life. She gritted her teeth if she heard Gladstone called "the People's William," the friend of ordinary workers.

Whenever she could, Victoria escaped to Balmoral, the scene of happier times with Prince Albert. She had written in her journal about those days, and in 1868 she published some of her recollections in a book. *Leaves from the Journal of Our Life in the Highlands*

The next prime minister, William Ewart Gladstone, championed equality and freedom and was unwilling to waver from the course he believed was right. He might have been a better politician, it was said, if he were not such a great man.

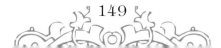

was bound in green cloth. In its pages the queen spoke about walks on wooded paths, boat rides, lakeside picnics, and evening games of whist. Victoria wrote about the "severe Highland scenery," which was stark and rocky yet "so wild and grand." She described the stirring sight of Scottish men dancing at night by torchlight, their feet never touching the sharp swords that lay crossed on the ground beneath them.

Many Britons wrote to their queen to tell her that they liked her book. Others went through its pages and counted how many times she mentioned a certain servant, John Brown. The answer was astonishing: twenty-one. The queen was so often with this big, bearded, handsome man that people were gossiping. What was going on?

As a *ghillie,* or outdoor servant, Brown had gone with Prince Albert on fishing and hunting trips at Balmoral. Albert had trusted him, and so did Victoria. She felt safe in his presence, and she relied on him more and more when she was in Scotland. Soon she would go on carriage rides only if Brown went along. In 1865 she promoted him and gave him a raise. As "the Queen's Highland Servant," Brown attended to her inside the castle and on its grounds, and she sometimes commanded his presence at Osborne and in London.

Visitors saw something other than a faithful subordinate. They saw an overpaid servant who had forgotten his station and was throwing his weight around. Brown quarreled with nearly everyone: Prince Alfred, the estate manager at Balmoral, the queen's chaplain, and her cabinet ministers. Once, when Gladstone was lecturing the queen, Brown cut him off with the curt words "You've said enough." This was shocking behavior, yet Brown was never reprimanded.

Servants could work for one family for many years, but they were never to think of themselves as their employers' equal. A double wall of class and custom divided them from the people who paid their salaries. Employers were to set a useful example of high moral standards. "Masters and mistresses cannot be too guarded in their own conduct so far as it may affect their servants," counseled a guidebook

from the Victorian era. For a well-to-do woman to single out a male servant as a favorite went beyond the limits of propriety. For the queen of England to do so was outrageous. Nevertheless, Queen Victoria let Brown live by his own rules. She overlooked his heavy drinking. She seemed not to notice if he puffed on his pipe, although she forbade the men in her family to smoke in her presence.

Rumors thrived. There were whispers that the relationship was sexual, or that the queen and Brown were married. Some people brazenly referred to Queen Victoria as Mrs. Brown. Gossips swore that the queen had secretly borne Brown's child. At the very least, she had "selected this man for a kind of friendship which is unwise and unbecoming in her position," said the Conservative statesman Lord Stanley. To this day, the true nature of Queen Victoria's relationship with John Brown remains unknown.

Victoria called Brown "a real treasure" and her best friend. "I have here always in the house, a good, devoted soul," she wrote to Vicky, "whose only object & interest is in my service." Her daughters thought differently. "He alone talks to her on all things, while we, her children, are restricted to speak on only things which do not excite her, or of which she chooses to talk," said a frustrated Princess Alice. Thinking about her own future household, Princess Louise stated, "I won't have an absurd man in a kilt following me about everywhere."

Alice and Louise never doubted that they would always have staffs of servants because the government supported all Queen Victoria's children. As her daughters married and her sons came of age, Victoria went to Parliament to request money for them. In 1871 she asked for an allowance for Prince Arthur, who was turning twenty-one. The same year, she sought a dowry for Princess Louise, who was to marry in March.

Louise was a gifted painter and sculptor. The most outspoken and independent of Victoria's daughters, she insisted on choosing her own husband. She took a long

Following pages: Wearing deep mourning, Queen Victoria reads old letters, presumably from Prince Albert. The servant holding her pony is John Brown.

time to make up her mind but at last accepted a proposal from a handsome Scottish nobleman, John Campbell, Marquess of Lorne. The wedding would be the first since 1515 between a daughter of a queen or king and a British subject not of royal blood. The match offered Britain no diplomatic advantages, but Queen Victoria defended it nonetheless. Times were changing, she said. Foreign alliances through marriage were becoming less important. She approved the choice "*for* Louise's happiness and for the peace and quiet of the family," she said.

Were Louise to marry a German prince, arguments would have broken out among her brothers and sisters. In 1870, a brief war in Europe had angrily divided the royal siblings. The Franco-Prussian War seemed engineered by Prussia's chancellor, Otto von Bismarck, to rid the German states of French influence. He planned to unite the separate states into the single nation that Albert had foreseen, and he would succeed. Like most people in Britain, Bertie and Alix favored Prussia's adversary, France. But as wife of the crown prince of Prussia, Vicky was firmly on the opposing side. Publicly Queen Victoria stayed neutral, but privately she sided with the Prussians, at least at first. Then reports reached her of German forces marching through neutral Belgium and butchering civilians by the thousands. "This frightful bloodshed is really too horrible in Europe in the 19th century," she thought, and she transferred her loyalty to the French. After France surrendered, she welcomed the exiled Napoleon III and his family into England.

Many British subjects viewed Princess Louise's marriage to one of their own as a sign of patriotism. "A feeling of satisfaction pervaded the country," wrote one journalist. "At last a stop was put to the practice of handing over our Princesses to petty German princelings."

Still, there were those who called Louise a "daughter of the horse-leech" and her future husband a "vampyre" feeding off the nation. A thirty-thousand-pound dowry for Princess Louise and another six thousand for her every year after that added up to a lot of money. And then there was the fifteen thousand pounds a year granted to Prince Arthur. All this was on top of the thousands that the British were already

Princess Louise and Prince Arthur. The queen's request for Parliament to provide financially
for them triggered a national debate over the cost of supporting the royal family.

paying to support the queen and the rest of her family. How was it, citizens asked, that Britain spent £637,000 every year on its royalty while it cost the United States the equivalent of £5,000 to maintain the president?

Parliament granted the money Victoria asked for, but in Birmingham and other cities, working people debated the cost of the monarchy. "They regard Prince Arthur as an able-bodied young man asking to be maintained out of the Imperial taxes," explained one reporter. The workers knew that if their own sons sought public funds, they would be asked: "Is there no sort of labour by which you can support yourselves, or have you no parents in sufficiently good circumstances to support you?" People thought Prince Arthur should face the same questions.

The press claimed that if people saw their taxes going toward something useful—if they saw the queen out in public doing her job—their anger might lessen. "Her Majesty has done much" to cause the discontent, stated a newspaper in far-off Australia. "She has suffered herself to glide almost imperceptibly out of notice." The writer concluded, "The country is not in a good temper."

CHAPTER X

A TALE OF TWO PRIME MINISTERS

IN NOVEMBER 1871, the Prince of Wales fell dangerously ill. Britons forgot their grudge against the queen and saw her as a woman, the best-known mother in the land. They worried about her son, their future king.

Politics and commerce halted as people waited for news from the prince's doctors. "Throughout India, in the Colonies, and even in the United States, the daily progress of the disease was recorded and watched," the *Times* noted. Most of Bertie's brothers and sisters hurried to Sandringham, his country cottage, and so did his distraught mother. The queen sat at her oldest son's bedside, quietly and tenderly, while her other children quarreled like youngsters. "Really the way in which they all squabble and wrangle and abuse each other destroys one's peace," complained one of Princess Alix's ladies in waiting.

Bertie had typhoid fever, which is transmitted through contaminated food and water. Typhoid attacks the blood, the airways, and the digestive tract. The danger comes from complications, such as a perforated intestine, which can be fatal. Bertie passed in and out of consciousness as his fever soared to 104 degrees. In his delirium he said crazy things. He thought he was king and was going to order the

Earl of Onslow (a future governor of New Zealand) to wear tights. The prince would rally one day only to have doctors declare him near death the next. "I hardly knew how to pray aright, only asking God if possible to spare my Beloved Child," Victoria wrote.

December 14 dawned. It was the tenth anniversary of the day Albert died. Queen Victoria had a dreadful feeling that Bertie would be called to Heaven on this date as well. But he survived, and the next day he was alert and able to kiss his mother's hand. "Oh! dear Mama, I am so glad to see you," he said. "Have you been here all this time?" Clearly, the crisis had passed. Relieved that her son would get well, Victoria understood how much he meant to her.

The queen had blamed Bertie for Albert's death. As he regained his health over the next two months, her conscience bothered her. She wanted to be closer to Bertie, but she refused to admit that she had been wrong. Instead she decided that since his illness Bertie had changed. He was "gentler and kinder than ever," she informed Vicky. "And there is something different which I can't exactly express. It is like a new life."

Now, if only Gladstone would leave her alone. The prime minister was calling for a grand celebration of the Prince of Wales's recovery, complete with a procession through London. Victoria's subjects wanted to rejoice along with the royal family that the prince was well again. What was more important, they needed to see her carrying out her official duties. Getting the queen to go out in public was a constant headache for Gladstone. Victoria balked at the thought of being part of such a show, but Princess Alix was pushing for it too, so she reluctantly agreed to go along.

On February 27, 1872, she rode in an open carriage with Bertie, Alix, their son Albert Victor, and Beatrice. They passed beneath banners and flags, with church bells ringing and spectators waving. "From the highest to the poorest 'rags,' there was but one and the same feeling!" Victoria remarked. The *Times* reported that Her Majesty "had a smile and a bow for every one." Said the fifty-two-year-old queen, "It was, of course very fatiguing—bowing all this time."

THANKSGIVING DAY, FEB. 27, 1872: THE PROCESSION APPROACHING ST. PAUL'S CATHEDRAL.

The royal carriage makes its way to St. Paul's Cathedral on the national thanksgiving day.
The Prince of Wales tips his hat to the joyful people who have come out to wish
him well. The prince's son Albert Victor sits between him and Princess Alix. Sitting across
from them are Queen Victoria and Princess Beatrice, who is dressed in blue.

The national thanksgiving day was "a great holyday for the people" and "an event for ever remarkable in the history of England," trumpeted the *Times.* It should have satisfied Gladstone, but all too soon, thought the queen, he was bothering her again. He pointed out that foreign dignitaries who visited England and expected to find hospitality at Windsor Castle were going home feeling snubbed. The king of Sweden, Prince Humbert of Italy, and others had to find their own lodgings and places to dine because Queen Victoria refused to entertain them.

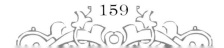

Why should she have to host "all Foreign Potentates WHO *chose* to come here for their own amusement," and at her own expense, Victoria asked. She did invite the queen of Hawaii to visit, but at three in the afternoon, so she would be gone before dinner. (Monarchs ruled the Kingdom of Hawaii from 1795 until 1893, when the United States annexed the Hawaiian islands.)

In spring 1873, Naser al-Din, the shah of Persia, was to visit Great Britain. Gladstone understood that it was essential to treat him with courtesy and respect. The shah's trip was a chance for Britain to form an important friendship in the Middle East, so Queen Victoria simply had to welcome him.

How the queen complained! She had heard rumors, she said, that the shah was "uncivilized," that he wiped his hands on other gentlemen's coattails and drank from the spout of a teapot. She had been told that he made improper remarks to ladies and ate with his hands while sitting on the floor. She instructed her household staff to lay down a spare carpet in the shah's bedchamber if it looked as if he might consume food there.

Not knowing what to expect, Victoria felt nervous on the day she met the shah. She hoped to bolster her confidence by looking regal, so she wore her finest jewels. They included the Koh-i-Noor diamond, which weighed more than a hundred carats and came from India. The shah was equally dazzling, with jewels studding his jacket, sword, and hat. Victoria noticed that he was "fairly tall and not fat, has a fine countenance and is very animated." He was anything but shy.

The shah surprised his hostess with his dignity and courtly manners. At lunch—which he ate with a fork and knife—he charmed the queen by praising her book, *Leaves from the Journal of Our Life in the Highlands*. He had had it translated into Persian so he could read it. "There was nothing to shock one at all in his eating or anything else," Victoria later reported to Vicky. She bestowed on the shah a British honor, the Order of the Garter. She also gave him a miniature portrait of herself. The state visit came off well, but Gladstone was not to suppose the queen would entertain every foreign leader who came to London.

Queen Victoria greets the shah of Persia, Naser al-Din, upon his arrival at Windsor Castle.

Life went on. Twelve years after Albert's death, Victoria was starting to smile again. In January 1874 she traveled to St. Petersburg, Russia, for the wedding of her son Alfred and Grand Duchess Marie Alexandrovna, the daughter of Tsar Alexander II. Alfred sported a full sea captain's beard, because he was an officer in the Royal Navy who had sailed as far as China and Australia. He and his bride planned to make their home in England.

A military career was fine for Alfred and his brother Arthur, but Victoria insisted that her youngest son follow a different, safer path. The queen had worried about Leopold all his life and had tried to protect him from injuries that might cause dangerous bleeding. Leopold had grown into a studious young man who liked

music, foreign languages, art, and literature. "His mind and head are far the most like of any of the boys' to his dear Father," Victoria thought. Yet Leopold had had to fight with his mother to attend college at Oxford. She gave in only after he promised to come home on weekends and go to Osborne at Easter and Balmoral in May. He would be at school to learn and not to have fun. "You fancy you are stronger than you really are," she told him.

Leopold completed his studies easily. Victoria then put him to work at her side, helping her stay up to date on foreign affairs. Twenty-one-year-old Leopold was of two minds about his new duties. He had hoped for a more public life, but he also found the work exceedingly interesting. He settled in to his role, although it meant dealing every day with his anxious, hovering mother. Victoria also had a life plan for her daughter Beatrice, her "Baby." Beatrice was never to marry. Instead she was to remain with the queen to help and keep her company.

The year 1874 gave Queen Victoria another reason to smile: the Liberal Party lost a national election. Gladstone's time as prime minister was over; at sixty-four, he was ready to retire. To Victoria's delight, Disraeli was back in. His manner, which Victoria described as "full of poetry, romance and chivalry," was a healing tonic to the lonely queen. Gladstone, she said, was "so very arrogant, tyrannical and obstinate with no knowledge of the world or human nature."

During his second ministry, Disraeli worked on strengthening Britain's position in the world. He viewed England as more than merely one of the European powers. "She is the metropolis of a great maritime empire, extending to the boundaries of the farthest ocean," he said grandly. In 1875 he arranged the purchase of a controlling share in the Suez Canal from the khedive, or governor, of Egypt. Completed in 1869, the canal allowed ships to travel between the Mediterranean and Red Seas by taking a shortcut through Egypt, avoiding the long trip around

In St. Petersburg, Russia, Prince Alfred escorts his bride, Grand Duchess Marie, to the wedding chapel.

Queen Victoria depended on her daughter Beatrice for help and companionship.

Africa that had been necessary before. The purchase ensured that British ships sailing to eastern colonies would have access to the canal.

In 1876 Disraeli persuaded Parliament to pass the Royal Styles and Titles Act, which gave Queen Victoria a second title, empress of India. Disraeli wanted to create a stronger bond between the monarchy and Britain's empire and tie India more tightly to the mother country. He also understood that the new title would boost the queen's popularity with the British people, for whom the empire was a source of pride. It pleased Queen Victoria, too, enough that she again opened Parliament in 1877. She thanked Disraeli by bestowing on him a title, Earl of Beaconsfield.

Victoria, queen of the United Kingdom of Great Britain and Ireland
and empress of India, adorned in her royal ermine robe.

She also displayed her friendship for Disraeli by lunching at his country home, Hughenden. To be a guest of the prime minister was an unusual thing for a queen or king to do. Every spring, she sent him a gift of primroses, his favorite flowers. The gallant Disraeli always thanked her profusely. In 1876 he wrote that he liked primroses "so much better for their being wild." They seemed "an offering from the Fauns and Dryads of the woods of Osborne."

The biggest issue Disraeli faced during his second ministry was the one people called the Eastern Question. Turkey's Ottoman Empire was declining. Violence was breaking out between Muslims and Christians in parts of the Balkan Peninsula that had once been firmly under Turkish control. In spring 1876, when Bulgarian Christians rose up, Turkey sent in troops known as *bashi-bazouk*s. These unruly soldiers and adventurers descended on Christian settlements and massacred some thirty thousand men, women, and children. The British people read about Bulgarian villages with silent sawmills and rotting harvests because the population had been wiped out. They read of heaps of bones, a blind boy who had been burned alive, and children whose heads had been split open with bayonets. "There was not a house beneath the ruins of which we did not perceive human remains," wrote a reporter on the scene.

Disraeli thought the accounts were overblown; Queen Victoria was inclined to believe them. How Britain should respond was a delicate problem, though. Two decades after the Crimean War, Russia still hungered for power in the Balkan countries. In Disraeli's view, a strong Turkey was the best deterrent against Russian aggression in the region. He also hoped to avoid drawing Great Britain into another war in that part of the world. He felt it was better for Britain not to intervene on behalf of the suffering Bulgarians.

Then, suddenly, Gladstone emerged from retirement to publish a scathing pamphlet, *Bulgarian Horrors and the Question of the East.* He accused the British government of knowing about the atrocities but keeping silent. He pointed out that

Britain had ambassadors in Turkey; they had to be aware of what was going on. By not taking action, the government was condoning the massacre, Gladstone asserted. "I entreat my countrymen," he wrote, "to require, and to insist, that our Government, which has been working in one direction, shall work in the other, and shall apply all its vigour . . . in obtaining the extinction of the Turkish power in Bulgaria." Only in this way, Gladstone wrote, could the world prevent "another murderous harvest, from the soil soaked and reeking with blood."

Gladstone the idealist had attacked the policy of Disraeli the practical man, and Queen Victoria was outraged. Gladstone, she swore, was a "half-madman," a "mischief-maker and firebrand." Disraeli added his own insults. He called Gladstone an "unprincipled maniac" and said that "of all Bulgarian horrors," his pamphlet was "perhaps the greatest." Gladstone's ideas proved popular, though. In just one month, two hundred thousand people bought his pamphlet. Crowds demonstrated in London, calling for Britain to send in soldiers.

Russia went to war with Turkey on April 24, 1877. Great Britain stayed out of the Russo-Turkish War, which ended ten months later in a Russian victory. Afterward, Disraeli took part in the 1878 Congress of Berlin, at which world powers recognized the independence of several Balkan nations and limited Russian influence in the region. A skillful negotiator, Disraeli secured for Great Britain the right to use Cyprus, an island off the Turkish coast, as a military base.

There were times when Disraeli—and Queen Victoria—sanctioned war, however. For a great empire to expand its reach was sometimes a brutal business. In 1878 British forces invaded Afghanistan with the goal of halting Russian influence there.

In November of that year, the military operation in Afghanistan was just getting started. Three thousand miles away, in the palace at Hesse-Darmstadt, Germany, Princess Alice's children began complaining of sore throats. One by one, they came down with diphtheria. Gray membranes grow in the throats of people with this

The British gained control over Afghanistan's foreign relations and promised the Central Asian nation freedom from outside domination. The Third Gurkha Rifles, an Indian infantry regiment, fought for Britain in Afghanistan.

highly contagious bacterial disease, and their necks can swell to an enormous size. Both symptoms can choke off a person's airway, making breathing difficult or impossible. Soon five of Alice's six children and her husband had fallen ill. Alice nursed them around the clock. The family's doctor told her not to kiss or hug anyone, because she needed to avoid getting sick herself.

Alas, diphtheria claimed Alice's youngest child, four-year-old May. Breaking the news to her son, ten-year-old Ernest, Alice forgot the doctor's rule and embraced the sorrowful boy. It was a fatal mistake. That brief contact was enough to infect Alice.

She died on December 14, 1878, the seventeenth anniversary of Prince Albert's death.

The German emperor issued an order that no one was to attend the funeral, to prevent the spread of infection. Queen Victoria stayed away, but her sons Bertie and Leopold, along with Helena's husband, Prince Christian, defied the decree and represented Alice's family at the service. Losing Alice left Queen Victoria feeling worn out and cast off. "[It had] aged and shaken the elasticity out of me," she wrote in her journal. When she turned sixty the following May, she noted, "It was a sad birthday, but I feel much and am cheered by the kindness of those left on earth. The other dear ones, my beloved Husband & our darling child, surely bless me."

Soon Great Britain was again at war, this time as part of a campaign to unite South Africa. The British had claimed territory in the region as early as 1795, but they coveted the land of their Dutch colonist neighbors, who were known as Afrikaners, or Boers, and of African tribal kingdoms, such as the Zulus. The 1879 conflict, known as the Zulu War, is remembered for its bloody clashes, especially the Battle of Isandlwana, fought on January 22. On that date some twenty thousand Zulu warriors killed more than half of a British force numbering twenty-two hundred. The queen blamed the loss at Isandlwana on the size of the British army there. It was "a lesson *never* to reduce our forces," she told Disraeli, "for, with our enormous Empire, we must always be prepared for such contingencies." The queen never mentioned that a thousand Zulus died in the battle as well. By July, Britain had won the war and robbed the Zulu people of their independence.

Were wars like these necessary? A loud, zealous voice was insisting they were not. "The foreign policy of England should always be inspired by the love of freedom," said none other than William Gladstone. The nation was soon to hold an election, and he was campaigning to return to government. His opposition to Disraeli's policies had lured him back into public life. He was traveling from one city to another, giving fiery speeches at every stop. Thousands came out to hear him speak

about the equality of all nations and the people who inhabited them. "The sanctity of life in the hill villages of Afghanistan among the winter snows, is as inviolable in the eye of Almighty God as can be your own," he reminded listeners. Newspapers printed his speeches, bringing them to a wider audience.

With such strong words, Gladstone won his way back into government. He also helped other Liberals gain votes, enough to achieve a majority in Parliament. This meant there would again be a change of prime ministers for Queen Victoria and

A political cartoonist who believed that Disraeli's policies harmed the poorer classes welcomed the rising sun of Gladstone's leadership.

the nation. It was Disraeli's turn to step down. He had lived for three-quarters of a century and had devoted most of his years to government. By 1880 his health was fragile; his wife, whom he had dearly loved, was dead. With a sad heart Victoria parted with the man she called "the kindest and most devoted as well as one of the wisest Ministers" she had ever known.

She steeled herself to deal again with Gladstone, "who would soon ruin everything, and be a *Dictator,*" as she claimed. Victoria issued instructions to Gladstone. First, she said, "There must be no democratic leaning." The queen worried that encouraging social equality might lead to uprisings such as the ones that had forced French leaders to flee their country. There was also to be "no attempt to change the Foreign policy . . . no change in India, no hasty retreat from Afghanistan . . . in short, no *lowering* of the *high position* the country holds, and *ought always* to hold."

But Gladstone followed his own course and made the nation more democratic. His government passed the Married Women's Property Act, for example, which allowed wives to own and control what was rightfully theirs. Before the law was passed, a woman's wealth became her husband's property at the time of their wedding. If a couple divorced, the wife could be left impoverished. The new law permitted women to keep anything they owned prior to marriage and whatever wealth they might acquire after marrying. Gladstone also undid some of Disraeli's foreign policy, notably withdrawing British forces from Afghanistan.

The current government was the worst ever, Queen Victoria thought. Working with Gladstone was "a bitter trial," she said, "for there is no more disagreeable Minister to have to deal with." Disraeli was angry with his successor too. He picked up a pen and started to write a novel about a character modeled on Gladstone. The fictional Joseph Toplady Falconet is born into a wealthy family. He grows up to become an eloquent statesman, eager and earnest, but one with little imagination and no sense of humor.

Disraeli never finished his novel. Ill with asthma and bronchitis, he died on April 19, 1881. "I can scarcely see for my fast falling tears," Victoria wrote. She

Queen Victoria places a wreath at Disraeli's resting place as a crowd of his admirers looks on.

sent a wreath of primroses from Osborne for his funeral. Four days after he was laid to rest, she went with Beatrice to Hughenden and placed another wreath inside the vault that housed the remains of Disraeli and his wife.

It fell to Prime Minister Gladstone to recommend that the government erect a statue of Benjamin Disraeli, Lord Beaconsfield, in historic Westminster Abbey. Standing in the House of Commons, Gladstone praised his late rival's finest qualities: "his strength of will; his long-sighted persistency of purpose . . . and last, but not least, of all, his great parliamentary courage." Gladstone later admitted that uttering these respectful, generous words was one of the hardest things he had ever done.

CHAPTER XI

"THE QUEEN IS ENOUGH TO KILL ANYONE"

ILLNESS COMES ON quickly in the damp chill of early spring. On March 19, 1883, John Brown woke up at Windsor with a bad cold that worked its way into his chest. On Easter Sunday, March 25, Brown's fever soared, and he took to his bed in a castle tower. Without whiskey, he suffered delirium tremens, the shaking, sweating, and confusion caused by withdrawal from alcohol. On Tuesday, March 27, he sank into a coma, and that night he died.

Prince Leopold had the unwelcome task of giving his mother the bad news. She was numb with disbelief and "very miserable," she said. No one had told her how seriously ill Brown was. The queen poured her grief into letter after letter, addressed to anyone she thought might offer sympathy: Vicky, her young grandchildren, and the poet Alfred, Lord Tennyson. "I have lost my dearest best friend who no-one in this world can ever replace," she wrote. "The shock—the blow, the blank, the constant missing at every turn of the one strong, powerful reliable arm and head almost stunned me and I am truly overwhelmed." No one reached out to her in the way she wanted, though. The rest of her family agreed with Leopold,

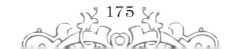

John Brown was photographed with Sharp, a border collie belonging to Queen Victoria.

who commented, "We can feel for her, & her sorrow, without being sorry for the cause." They were not going to miss John Brown.

The queen sent a wreath of white flowers to be placed on Brown's coffin. She commissioned a sculptor to create a life-size statue of Brown to grace the grounds of Balmoral. She had his portrait painted and hung in Windsor Castle. She ordered his room at Windsor kept just as it was, and a fresh flower placed every day on the pillow. She would do more.

In June 1884, Queen Victoria called on the Reverend Randall Davidson, who was newly appointed to St. George's Chapel at Windsor. She showed him some pages of a book she was writing, a memoir of John Brown that she intended to publish. Young and unused to counseling royalty, Davidson had no idea what to say. Did he dare tell the queen the truth, that this book would make her a laughingstock? He tried gently to change her mind and hoped he had succeeded. But soon Davidson received a worried letter from a Dr. Hamilton Lees of Edinburgh. Her Majesty had shown him her book at Balmoral, Dr. Lees wrote. Having it printed was "a most absurd fancy altogether, and I wish it would pass away," he stated. The queen was determined to proceed, and Lees wondered how she could be stopped.

Davidson had no choice but to speak frankly to Queen Victoria, which people almost never did. When he next saw her, he tried his best to sound firm but diplo-

matic. He commented that the public and the press had shared her grief when the prince consort died. They had a different attitude toward John Brown, however. "I feel I should be wanting in my honest duty to Your Majesty who has honoured me with some measure of confidence were I not to refer to this," he said. Victoria lost her temper and demanded an apology, but Davidson refused to take back his words. Instead, he offered to resign.

In time Victoria's anger cooled, and she thought the matter over. One day she called for Davidson and gave him a friendly welcome. She never mentioned the memoir again, to Davidson or anyone else. The incident had a happy ending for Davidson, who stayed on at St. George's Chapel for many years and in 1903 was appointed archbishop of Canterbury.

Another spring brought further anguish for Queen Victoria: the loss of a son. In March 1884, Prince Leopold traveled to the South of France, needing to rest in a warm climate for his health. Leopold loved the southern French coast; he planned to buy land there and build a seaside home for himself and his family. In 1882 Leopold had married Princess Helene of Waldek-Pyrmont, a German principality. They had a daughter, Alice, who was born in 1883, and Helene was pregnant again.

But there would be no house in France. On March 24, Leopold slipped while climbing stairs in his hotel, hitting his knee and head. For a person with hemophilia, a bruise or bump on the head can cause bleeding beneath the skin and be as deadly as an open wound. Leopold died four days later, at age thirty.

Queen Victoria wept for her lost son. "How dear Le was to me, how I watched over him. . . . The poor dear boy's life had been a very tried one, from early childhood. He was such a dear charming companion." She thought of "that poor loving young wife" and "how may this news affect her!" About herself, she said, "I am a poor desolate old woman, and my cup of sorrow overflows!" Bertie went to France and brought the body home for burial. Leopold's son, named Charles, was born four months later. He was the queen's thirty-second grandchild.

So much that happened was beyond a queen's control. Loved ones died, and

Britain mourned with Queen Victoria when Prince Leopold died. Leopold inherited hemophilia from his mother. A female will have the condition only if the trait is passed on from both of her parents, whereas a male only needs to inherit it from one. A woman like Queen Victoria, with one gene for hemophilia, is called a carrier: she can pass along the condition but shows no signs or symptoms herself. Princess Alice, Princess Beatrice, and Leopold's daughter, Alice, were carriers as well. Hemophilia appeared in descendants of theirs among the Russian, Spanish, and German royalty.

young people lived their own lives. In 1884 Beatrice surprised her mother with the news that she wanted to marry. While visiting Germany she had fallen in love with dashing Prince Heinrich of Battenberg, who was an officer in the Prussian army. Queen Victoria was not amused. A husband for Beatrice was not in her plans. With John Brown and Leopold gone, she needed Baby beside her more than ever. For the next seven months she said not one word to Beatrice, hoping that her displeasure would put an end to the whole notion of a wedding.

Beatrice and Heinrich remained firm through those months, and in the end it was Queen Victoria who gave in. She would give the couple her blessing, she said, but only if Beatrice lived with her husband in Buckingham Palace. She was to remain her mother's companion, and Heinrich was to leave the army and be known as Prince Henry. Grateful for the queen's consent, the two agreed to her terms and were married on July 23, 1885, in a church near Osborne. Beatrice wore the queen's wedding veil.

Gladstone, too, was beyond Queen Victoria's control. Despite his outcries against war, he had let Britain be drawn into military conflicts when its interests abroad were threatened. In 1882, for example, he sent soldiers to put down

an uprising in Egypt. The rebellion dragged on and stretched south into Sudan, where a loyal Egyptian garrison and a number of British subjects found themselves trapped in the city of Khartoum.

Subject to Egyptian administration since the 1820s, Sudan was a dry, hot, inhospitable land. Khartoum, however, sat at a fertile place on the life-giving Nile River. Its white minaret rose above the tops of palm trees, and its houses built of mud sat amid tropical foliage. It was a busy, noisy port, where enslaved laborers loaded boats bound for European markets with ivory and acacia gum.

Gladstone believed his nation had a duty to protect its citizens and the Egyptian troops, so in January 1884, he sent Major General Charles Gordon to the region. Gordon was a popular choice, a celebrated adventurer who loved to do battle. He had long been a soldier in foreign places, and from 1877 to 1880, he was governor general of Sudan. He had clear orders to assess the situation and advise the government; he was to do nothing more.

If there was a drawback to sending Gordon on this mission, it was his inclination to act on his own, as though he answered to no one. Upon reaching Khartoum he evacuated twenty-five hundred women and children and sent them safely to Egypt. In this instance, Gordon's independence had served him well. Then he decided to defend Khartoum. It was a foolhardy move because military leaders were withdrawing British and Egyptian units from other parts of Sudan. Alone, with no nearby reinforcements, Gordon and his forces faced the army of Muhammad Ahmad, a Sudanese religious teacher who had proclaimed himself the Mahdi, or defender of Islam. The Mahdi was determined to rid Sudan of Egyptian (and British) influence.

For month after month Gordon and his men held off the Mahdi's soldiers. They waited desperately for aid from Britain, but Gladstone was slow to send it. In his view, Gordon had acted against orders, and the Mahdi and his people were patriots "struggling rightly to be free." From Balmoral a frustrated Victoria bombarded Gladstone with letters, urging him to take action. "The Queen trembles for General Gordon's safety," she wrote. When Gladstone finally did send a relief force, it was

Muhammad Ahmad, the Mahdi, believed
he was an Islamic spiritual leader. He fought
against outside governance in Sudan.

too late. It reached Khartoum on January 28, 1885, only to find that the city had fallen, the trapped Egyptian soldiers had been slaughtered, and Gordon had been stabbed to death.

Victoria was horrified and outraged. She sent telegrams to Gladstone, to the war minister, and to the foreign secretary, all bearing the same words: "To think that all this might have been prevented and many precious lives saved by earlier action is too frightful." There was nothing secure about sending information over the telegraph lines, as Victoria knew. Operators between Balmoral and London intercepted the queen's message, and in this way the public learned of Her Majesty's displeasure with Gladstone and his government. Now it was Gladstone's turn to be angry. "The Queen is enough to kill anyone," he complained. He vowed never to set foot in Windsor Castle again, which was fine with Victoria. "He will be for ever branded with the blood of Gordon that heroic man," she declared.

An issue close to Gladstone's heart was independence for Ireland. In 1800 Parliament had passed the Act of Union, making Ireland part of Great Britain. Since then, many Irish had been demanding separation from the mother country and a legislature of their own—what they called Home Rule. Theirs was a largely Roman Catholic country led by Protestants who often discriminated against people of the Catholic faith. They had watched elite English landlords profit off Ireland's land while its people lived in poverty. They had painful memories of the Great Famine of

the 1840s and 1850s, when a million people died and the British government withheld needed aid. Violent clashes were taking place in Ireland between the nationalists—those who favored Home Rule—and the unionists—those who wanted to remain part of Britain's United Kingdom.

Gladstone had long fought in Parliament for the Irish people and their rights. By the 1880s he was convinced that Ireland deserved Home Rule. "When once he had convinced himself of any subject, it ceased to be his opinion, and became a cosmic truth," commented a gentleman who knew him. "He was working not for his own idea but for some great cause external to him." In 1886 Gladstone introduced his Home Rule Bill in Parliament, but it got too few votes to pass. "I cannot help feeling relieved," Queen Victoria wrote in her journal, "and think it is best for the country." She worried that Irish Home Rule might lead to instability in other parts of the United Kingdom.

Gladstone's 1886 resignation after the defeat of his bill also brought Victoria relief. At seventy-six the "Grand Old Man" of British politics was indeed old and looked unwell. The queen let out a big, happy sigh, sure that her days of working with him were over.

She got along splendidly with the next prime minister, Robert Gascoyne-Cecil, Marquess of Salisbury, who was a Conservative. Salisbury was a tremendous man—six feet, four inches tall and portly, with a bushy gray beard.

An artist imagined General Gordon's death in Khartoum.

In this political cartoon, angry men kick Gladstone and his failed Home Rule Bill into the air.

He was an aristocrat who traced his lineage back for centuries. In the 1600s his ancestors had advised Queen Elizabeth I and King James I. Victoria's friendship with Salisbury was founded on mutual respect. She praised him as "one of the most intelligent and large minded and unprejudiced statesmen" she'd ever known. Salisbury perceived that beneath her moodiness and obstinate nature, the queen possessed good judgment. "She had an extraordinary knowledge of what her people would think," he said. "I have always felt that when I knew what the Queen thought, I knew pretty certainly what view her subjects would take."

In 1887 the Royal Society of Arts gave its Albert Medal to Queen Victoria. Created in 1864 to honor Prince Albert, the medal rewards "distinguished merit in promoting arts, manufactures, or commerce." In honoring the queen, "the personal embodiment of the nation," the society was recognizing the great changes that had occurred during her fifty years on the throne.

Fifty years! Those five decades had brought comfort and convenience to Britain's middle and upper classes. In 1887, many of their homes were wired for electricity, and some boasted telephones. Photography had become a popular pastime among the rich. Not everyone enjoyed such ease, however. Immigrants who

had fled poverty and persecution in eastern Europe now crowded London's East End. They competed for work with poor, uprooted farm laborers. With the economy in recession, jobs eluded thousands of willing workers, foreign and native-born alike. In 1887, 250,000 people left Britain to seek better lives in Australia, New Zealand, or North America.

Most Britons admired the queen, but others scorned her. She was brazenly booed, for example, when she opened a music hall in East London. More than a hundred Liberal Party members refused to stand when she was toasted at a formal dinner. Still, only three other English monarchs had reigned for half a century. Henry III was king from 1216 until 1272; Edward III ruled from 1327 until 1377; and Victoria's grandfather George III was king from 1760 until 1820. Politics aside, Queen Victoria's Golden Jubilee was something to celebrate.

Not if it meant appearing in public, the queen protested. She was tired, and her back ached. She used a walking stick for support, and when fatigued she sank into her rolling chair. These were just excuses, government ministers and her children countered. They pleaded with her to reconsider. Well, all right, Victoria said at last, but she would not wear a crown or anything fancy. A plain black dress—the same style that had served her well since 1861—would be just fine. No, insisted the others. "Now, Mother, you must have something really smart," her son Alfred said, speaking for all.

So on June 21, when a royal procession once again left Buckingham Palace, Queen Victoria wore a lacy white bonnet. The carriages wended their way past shouting admirers to Westminster Abbey, which Victoria had last entered as a young woman of nineteen, on the day of her coronation.

A college student seated somewhere in the high tiers that lined the historic church rose to his feet with the rest of the crowd as kings, queens, princes, and princesses entered and took their seats. "After the jewels and the robes and the uniforms had flashed by, there moved up one solitary little figure in a black satin

THE QUEEN'S JUBILEE THANKSGIVING FESTIVAL IN LONDON, TUESDAY, JUNE 21.

ARRIVAL OF THE QUEEN AT THE WEST DOOR OF WESTMINSTER ABBEY.

The queen arrives at Westminster Abbey for the religious service marking her Golden Jubilee.

dress with a white front and a white bonnet," he remembered. "She was Queen of England and Empress of India . . . and there she was, a little old lady coming to church to thank God for the long years in which she had ruled her people."

While a choir sang to music Prince Albert had arranged, the college student noticed her hand trembling. Victoria's thoughts were drifting to the past, to people she had loved and lost. She felt "great pain," she said, recalling "above all, the dear husband and father, two dear children, my dear Mother," and many others. She remembered John Brown, "the loyalest, best friend who so loyally and lovingly looked after me!"

The queen was wistful, but her subjects felt festive. They snatched up mementos, among them souvenir medals, commemorative books, and teapots and plates bearing the likeness of Queen Victoria. They came out for parades, fireworks, and parties. Soldiers lined up for review. To honor this milestone in the queen's life, the women of Great Britain collected seventy thousand pounds, which they presented to Her Majesty to use for whatever purpose she chose. Still an admirer of Florence Nightingale's, Victoria founded a nursing school. Queen Victoria's Jubilee Institute for Nurses trained women to care for the sick poor.

Candles light up the night as Queen Victoria, her family, and guests enjoy a state banquet at Buckingham Palace celebrating her fifty years on the throne.

Using the money to help her needy subjects was a generous, sensible act on the part of a woman who was also capable of behaving unreasonably—as her family and associates knew all too well. In later life she formed a close friendship that maddened nearly all of them. It was with Abdul Karim, a new waiter at Windsor. He had been born in India, the son of a hospital assistant attached to the British army. Like the queen's other Indian servants, he wore turbans, golden sashes, and long, skirted coats: blue at breakfast, white at dinner in summer, and red in winter. Upon meeting Karim, Victoria decided that this tall, handsome twenty-four-year-old deserved to be more than an ordinary servant. She made him a secretary, although he barely knew how to read and write. Everyone was to call him the Munshi, a Hindi title meaning "scribe" or "clerk." He was often at the queen's side.

To Queen Victoria he may have been "zealous, attentive and quiet and gentle," a man with "intelligence and good sense." But others saw Abdul Karim as someone putting on airs. In the royal household, people were acutely aware of their position in the hierarchy. The queen's personal secretary, her physician, and her ladies in waiting took offense at having to dine with the Munshi, in their eyes a mere servant, and treat him as an equal. They resented seeing him seated in a place of honor at social events. Victoria's children and advisors threw up their hands in frustration. If they tried to reason with the queen about the favoritism she showed toward Karim, she accused them of prejudice. They had no regard for "the poor Munshi's sensitive feelings."

The prime minister counseled everyone to have patience. After all, the Munshi presented a threat to no one. Salisbury suspected that the queen merely wanted to stir up a little harmless trouble. As he explained to Dr. James Reid, who became the queen's medical attendant in 1881, "She really likes the emotional excitement, as being the only form of excitement she can have."

Karim accompanied Queen Victoria when she traveled overseas. Victoria had started going abroad in summer, to France, Switzerland, Germany, or Italy. The woman who had once traipsed around Paris during a stifling August now needed to

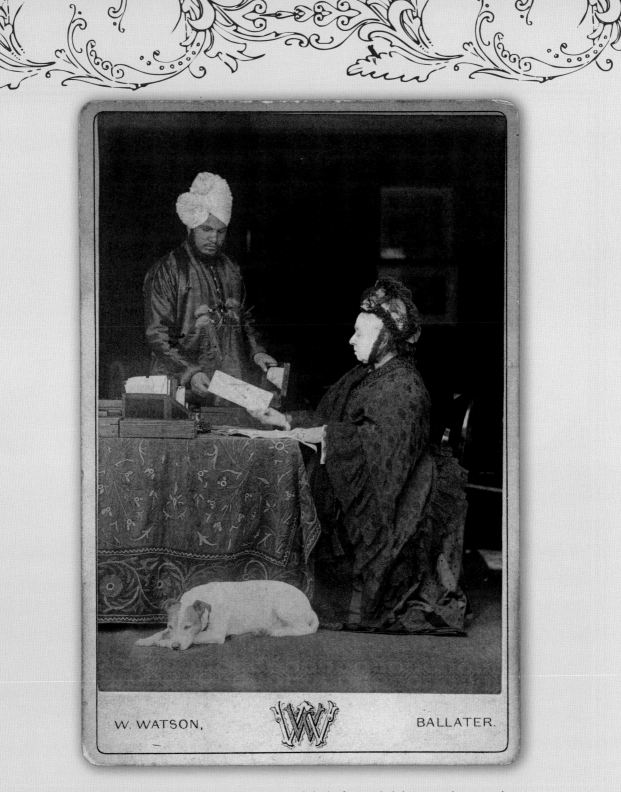

Queen Victoria conducts business with help from Abdul Karim, the man she called the Munshi. A terrier rests at her feet; Queen Victoria loved dogs all her life.

Queen Victoria sits on the terrace of the Villa Palmieri, in central Italy, a place she visited three times. Two Indian servants stand in attendance. The queen spent many hours at work whenever she traveled.

escape London's heat. It was worse for her than it was for everyone else because she never perspired. Or so she claimed.

So that her every need was met, Queen Victoria brought along a large staff: servants and secretaries, doctors and a dentist, and a French chef and his assistants. She often booked an entire hotel to provide each person a room. She brought her bed and desk, favorite pictures, trunks and trunks of clothes, carriages, and the horses and ponies to pull them. Once across the English Channel, everyone and everything was loaded onto Queen Victoria's private train.

She owned two railroad cars that were stored at a station in Belgium to be ready for her to use in Europe. Inside one was a drawing room with blue, yellow, and pearl-colored silk hanging on its walls. It held a sofa, chairs, and footstools, all carved, gilded, and fringed. The other was a sleeping car. The queen's train stopped for an hour every morning while she dressed, and again at mealtimes. European rail lines adjusted their timetables to accommodate England's queen.

In 1889 she was the first reigning English monarch to visit Spain. She made three trips to Florence, Italy. Prince Albert had toured the city in his youth, and he was often in her thoughts.

Robert Gascoyne-Cecil, Lord Salisbury, was the last prime minister to become Queen Victoria's friend.

One day, an English boy who was also in Florence noticed policemen clearing traffic to let a small carriage enter the Piazza del Duomo, Florence's famed cathedral square. The boy recognized the woman in the carriage. "It was Queen Victoria," he said. He saw the queen open a locket that she wore around her neck. A lady in waiting explained to the boy that the locket held a miniature portrait of Prince Albert. The queen held it up, as if wishing she could share with her late husband the grandeur of the cathedral's marble arches and sculpted saints.

Victoria liked to holiday at Cimiez, in southern France. While there she often visited Lord Salisbury at his French vacation house. "I never saw two people get on better," said another of Salisbury's guests. "Their polished manners and deference to and esteem for each other were a delightful sight and one not readily to be forgotten." Salisbury's daughter Lady Gwendolen Cecil noted that, with the exception of ties to close family members, his friendship with the queen was "the warmest and closest of Lord Salisbury's life."

CHAPTER XII

THE
LAST PROCESSION

AUGUST 11, 1892, was a gloomy day for Queen Victoria. Lord Salisbury's Conservative Party had failed to win a majority in a recent election, and he resigned as prime minister. "These are trying moments," the queen said. She was sorry to part with Salisbury, but she was sorrier to entrust the government to the Liberal who replaced him. The politician leading the new majority in the House of Commons was "an old, wild, incomprehensible man of 82 ½," as she described him. With dismay she watched him "walking rather bent, with a stick . . . his face shrunk, deadly pale, with a weird look in his eye." Her old foe, Gladstone, was back.

Still determined to secure independence for Ireland, Gladstone introduced his Second Home Rule Bill in the House of Commons. The nationalists and unionists were so much at odds over the future of Ireland that the members of Parliament had a fistfight. "Hats were knocked off in all directions. The House filled with uproar," a newspaperman wrote. "A tumultuous mass of men clutched at each other's throats" as "hissing, booing, yelling roared through the House." The journalist reported that "one member was knocked down and dragged out of the scuffle by the

heels." Despite the torn coats and bruised faces, the House of Commons passed Gladstone's bill—only to see it struck down in the House of Lords. (Until 1911, the House of Lords had the power to approve or reject laws passed in the House of Commons.) The Irish were to wait another thirty-six years for independence. The Republic of Ireland would be established in 1922, after more than two years of bitter warfare. Then, Northern Ireland's remaining part of the United Kingdom led to protests and violent clashes that continued well into the twentieth century.

The defeat of his bill in the House of Lords helped persuade the aged prime minister to resign for the final time on March 2, 1894. Rather than thanking him for his service, Queen Victoria sent him a brusque letter stating that he was right to step down and stop straining his eyes. Gladstone confided to people close to him that his feelings were hurt.

An aged Gladstone introduces his Second Home Rule Bill in Parliament. Although Gladstone is considered one of Britain's great prime ministers, his reputation rests on his character and principles rather than on his skill at governing.

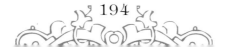

When he died, in May 1898, Victoria's family urged her to praise his achievements. "He was a great Englishman and it is fitting to do honour to his memory as such," Vicky counseled. Her mother disagreed. "He was a clever man, full of talent, but he never *tried* to keep up the *honour* and *prestige* of Great Britain," Queen Victoria responded. She recalled too many times when Gladstone's actions went against the national interest, as she saw it. He had criticized British policy toward Turkey; he had dallied when he should have rescued General Gordon; he had doggedly pursued Irish Home Rule. It angered her that Bertie and his son George served as pallbearers at Gladstone's funeral.

Queen Victoria called Gladstone old, but she too was no longer young. She was seventy-eight in 1897, when her country again celebrated her long reign. The Diamond Jubilee marked her sixtieth year on the throne. Andrew Carnegie, a captain of American industry, was in England at the time and witnessed the cheering, parades, and garden parties. "It is not possible for any American, however well informed of British affairs, to quite understand the feelings with which this human being is now regarded," Carnegie stated. An American would have to imagine "'Old Glory' and Old Ironsides, Washington and Lincoln, Bunker Hill and 'My Country, Tis of Thee,' rolled into one force, and personified in a woman."

Generations of Britons had been born and grown up with Victoria sitting on the throne. Among them was the science-fiction author H. G. Wells, whose mother was a devoted admirer of the queen's. "She followed the life of Victoria, her acts and utterances, her goings forth and her lyings in, her great sorrow and her other bereavements, with a passionate loyalty," Wells wrote. He told readers that his mother liked to imagine how she would behave if she were queen. "One would say this. One would do that. I have no doubt about my mother's reveries," Wells added. "In her latter years in a black bonnet and a black silk dress she became curiously suggestive of the supreme widow."

So long a recluse, Queen Victoria now liked appearing in public. A man who saw her speak at the opening of an exhibition described what he remembered:

HER MAJESTY'S GRACIOUS SMILE.

Charles Knight,
Court Photographer,
26, Queen's Road,
... Aldershot.

Sixty years on the throne is a reason to feel happy. Queen Victoria was photographed thousands of times. She, Albert, and their children were the first royal family to pose for a camera, and she liked the medium of photography. The earliest images, from the 1840s, are on the sensitized silver plates perfected by Louis Daguerre. These daguerreotypes are dark and difficult to see. At the end of her life, Victoria owned twenty thousand photographs, many of which are held at Windsor Castle. This is a rare one of a smiling Queen Victoria.

"The little black figure rose in her box, she addressed the vast assembly in that clear quiet voice which penetrated into every corner like a ray of light, and, when she had done, she made three low curtsies to her people." The queen still had a beautiful voice.

At home she doted on her grandchildren. They numbered thirty-eight, and some of them were grown up, married, and producing her great-grandchildren. "It seems to me to go on like the rabbits in Windsor Park!" she laughed. Victoria had been strict with her sons and daughters, but she let their offspring climb into her lap and play in her room. They rolled on the carpet and used boxes to build fortresses

around her feet. She and the children shared giggling carriage rides and picnic teas. The youngsters ran on palace grounds while she read reports and signed letters in the shade of a nearby tree. When the American showman Buffalo Bill brought his Wild West Show to England, Queen Victoria invited the troupe to Windsor to perform for the children.

The queen was also a grandmotherly figure for the men in Great Britain's armed forces. She knit them warm garments and sent them chocolate when they were deployed overseas. At the close of the nineteenth century, British troops were again fighting in South Africa. Once more they were battling the Afrikaners for land and control of the region. The conflict began badly for the British, who found their armies quickly surrounded or defeated. During an especially disastrous eight days in December 1899—a period remembered as Black Week—2,776 British fighting men were killed, wounded, or captured. But Queen Victoria refused to be discouraged. After a briefing at Windsor Castle she said, "Please understand that there is no one depressed in *this* house; we are not interested in the possibilities of defeat; they do not exist."

In the Orange River Trenches holding back the Boers—South Africa.
Copyright 1900 by Underwood & Underwood.

Trenches protect soldiers fighting in the Boer War. Hostilities continued until a 1902 treaty united South Africa under British rule. The Afrikaners retained their own language, Afrikaans, however, and their own customs and religion.

The queen poses
with three of her great-grandchildren.
Princess Mary, Prince Edward, and Prince Albert
were children of Bertie and Alix's son George,
the future King George V. The two little boys
would also grow up to reign,
as King Edward VIII and King George VI.

The queen who spoke those words soon had to weather life's last cruel blow: the death in 1900 of her son Alfred from cancer. She felt heartbroken to think of "this dear, excellent, gallant boy, beloved by all, such a good as well as a brave and capable officer, gone," she wrote. She sought consolation from Marie Mallet, one of her ladies of the bedchamber. "When she breaks down and draws me close to her and lets me stroke her dear hand I quite forget she is far above me and only realise she is a sorrowing woman who clings to human sympathy," Mallet told her husband. Queen Victoria cried silent tears, let her ladies comfort her, and carried on. "After the Prince Consort's death I wished to die," the queen confided to Mallet, "but *now* I wish to live and do what I can for my country and those I love."

As the world entered the twentieth century, the country Queen Victoria served was passing her by. She had no interest in new machines such as automobiles, typewriters, and telephones, which excited younger people. She was sleepy during the day and nodded off while her ladies read to her in the evening. Her eyesight was failing; her handwriting became impossible to read. She stopped keeping her journal.

She spent Christmas 1900 at Osborne House and lingered there into the new year. On January 16, 1901, Dr. Reid noticed that she appeared confused and had trouble speaking. He thought she had suffered a small stroke. Three days later, as the queen worsened, Reid summoned her family to Osborne. For the next couple of days, Bertie, Alix, Louise, Helena, and the others watched as she slipped in and out of consciousness. There were some moments when she recognized people and others when she mistook one person for another.

Vicky was ill with cancer and could not be with her mother, but her son Wilhelm, who adored his grandmother, rushed to be at her side. Following the deaths of his German grandfather and father, Wilhelm was now Kaiser, or emperor, of Germany. On the evening of January 22, Wilhelm was ushered into a bedchamber where an enormous painting of the dead Christ taken down from the cross hung over the fireplace. He heard the queen struggling to breathe. Dr. Reid had had her lifted into

a small bed, where she could more easily be nursed, and had ordered her big, solid mahogany double bed moved out of the room. Queen Victoria's eldest grandchild placed his arm around her shoulders. In his caring embrace, she died.

Wilhelm reflected on his grandmother's many years. She had been old enough to remember King George III, "and now we are in the Twentieth Century," he remarked. "And all that time what a life she has led. I have never been with her without feeling that she was in every sense my Grandmamma and made me love her as such. And yet the minute we began to talk about political things she made me feel we were equals and could speak as Sovereigns. Nobody had such power as she."

In Parliament the next day, Lord Salisbury, praised his friend the queen. "She reigned by sheer force of character, by the lovableness of her disposition, over the hearts of her subjects, and exercised an influence in moulding their character and destiny," Salisbury said. "She has been a great instance of government by example, by esteem, by love." He observed that Victoria's reign "bridged over that great interval which separates old England from new England." The nation made that transition smoothly thanks to "the tact, the wisdom, the passionate patriotism" of the late queen.

Already Queen Victoria belonged to the past; Great Britain had a new king. Bertie chose to reign as Edward VII instead of using his full name, Albert Edward. He wanted people to think only of the prince consort when they heard the name Albert. In this way, he said, he

Edward VII drives an automobile, showing that he is a king for the twentieth century.

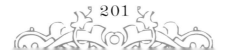

VICTORIA

LACHRYMÆ.

A female figure sheds tears for the departed queen
in this artist's expression of national grief.

honored his "great and wise Father." Victoria's death had closed the door on the Victorian era, and Britain entered a new period, the Edwardian age. Edward VII was to be a popular king, although, as his parents had feared, he was an unfaithful husband.

Queen Victoria had entrusted written instructions for her burial with Dr. Reid. He and an assistant followed them to the letter. In her coffin they placed objects that she had asked for, among them pieces of jewelry and photographs, Prince Albert's dressing gown, and the plaster cast of his hand. Into her left hand the doctor slipped a photograph of John Brown and a lock of Brown's hair. He covered these items with flowers before the queen's family viewed the body. The king invited Abdul Karim, his mother's Munshi, to say a final goodbye.

Royal processions had borne Queen Victoria through London all her life. Now a procession escorted her to the grave. She had requested a military funeral, so by custom her coffin traveled on a gun carriage pulled by cream-colored horses, like the team from her coronation day. A million spectators came together in the center of the city to honor their queen one last time. People poured out of railway cars. Many came on foot, having left home as early as four a.m. No sunshine warmed the backs of their black coats and cloaks. They stood for hours in piercing cold, bracing themselves against a keen, steady wind. Edward VII, an up-to-date king, had ordered a brief six-week national mourning period.

Thirty thousand solders lined the route. Sand had been spread on the streets to hush the thud of men's boots, the hollow knocking of horses' hooves, the clatter of carriage wheels. Silence prevailed, interrupted only by whispers of "the Queen! The Queen!" as the cloth-draped coffin passed. A train brought Queen Victoria's body to Windsor for the funeral in St. George's Chapel. It then lay in state for two days before being placed beside Albert in the mausoleum at Frogmore.

Most people were too young to remember a time without Queen Victoria on the throne. She was like a figure from a myth. She was also like someone in their family

whose quirks and foibles could get them upset but whose good qualities they treasured. The world "has ceased to believe in the Divine right of kings," commented one of her subjects. "But it will never cease to reverence that kingship, or queenship . . . which proves that it has the grace of God by possessing sweet human graces, and by showing throughout a whole lifetime, as our Victoria has done, that to be a true man or woman is the Royalest thing on earth."

One man wrote, "She had kindled the imagination of her people, as no other English monarch perhaps had ever done, and the throne had never been held in such love and reverence."

Yes, people loved her. After all, she represented Britain.

Guardsmen stand watch as the queen's body lies in state at Windsor Castle. A small crown adorns the cloths that drape the coffin.

GREAT BRITAIN'S LIMITED MONARCHY

THE PRIME MINISTER leads the government of the United Kingdom of Great Britain and Northern Ireland. He or she usually is the politician who heads a majority in the House of Commons. The prime minister selects the cabinet ministers, who oversee such areas as foreign affairs, national defense, the economy, and social services. The cabinet ministers also make up the Privy Council, which advises the queen or king.

Parliament, the nation's lawmaking body, comprises the House of Commons and the House of Lords. Men and women are elected to the House of Commons to represent their geographical constituencies. They are known as members of Parliament, or MPs. Those in the House of Lords are called peers. They have titles of nobility or are bishops or arch-bishops of the Church of England. They remain in Parliament for as long as they hold their titles, which can be for life. Bills are passed first in the House of Commons, following spirited debate. They move on to the House of Lords for further debate. If the peers vote their assent to passage, the bill is sent to the monarch, whose royal assent turns the bill into law.

When the nation holds a general election, every seat in the House of Commons is up for a vote. Members are elected for five-year terms, but not every Parliament lasts a full five years. A prime minister who sees that the nation no longer stands behind his or her policies loses the confidence of the legislators and the nation. Parliament can be dissolved and a new election will be held. This is what happened in 1886, for example, when Gladstone resigned after the defeat of his Home Rule Bill. Much later, in 2016, Prime Minister David Cameron resigned after Britain voted to leave the European Union (EU). Cameron had favored EU membership.

Britain considers its monarch to be head of state, but he or she plays a small role in governing and is expected to be neutral in politics. The queen or king does have certain powers, known as the royal prerogative. Among these is the power to appoint prime ministers. The monarch may also pardon convicted criminals, declare war, make treaties, deploy armed forces, and confer honors, titles, and decorations. In exercising the royal prerogative, the king or queen acts on the advice of the government ministers.

THE KINGS & QUEENS OF ENGLAND & GREAT BRITAIN

QUEEN VICTORIA BELONGED to a long line of monarchs who have worn the crown of England or Great Britain. There was one significant break in this lineage, beginning in 1649, following a civil war and the beheading of King Charles I. England was declared a republic and ruled by a lord protector, first the soldier and politician Oliver Cromwell and then his son, Richard Cromwell. The monarchy was restored in 1660, when Parliament proclaimed that the executed ruler's oldest son would be King Charles II.

MONARCH	YEARS OF REIGN
Egbert	802–39
Ethelwulf	839–58
Ethelbald	858–60
Ethelbert	860–66
Ethelred	866–71
Alfred the Great	871–99
Edward the Elder	899–924
Athelstan	924–39
Edmund the Magnificent	939–46
Edred	946–55
Edwy	955–59
Edgar the Peaceable	959–75

Edward the Martyr	975–78
Ethelred the Unready	979–1013 and 1014–16
Sweyn Forkbeard	1013–14
Edmund Ironside	1016
Canute	1016–35
Harold I	1035–40
Hardicanute	1040–42
Edward the Confessor	1042–66
Harold II	1066
William the Conqueror	1066–87
William II	1087–1100
Henry I	1100–1135
Stephen	1135–54
Empress Matilda (Queen Maud)	1141
Henry II	1154–89
Richard the Lionheart	1189–99
John	1199–1216
Henry III	1216–72
Edward I	1272–1307
Edward II	1307–27
Edward III	1327–77
Richard II	1377–99
Henry IV	1399–1413
Henry V	1413–22
Henry VI	1422–61
Edward IV	1461–83
Edward V	1483
Richard III	1483–85
Henry VII	1485–1509

Henry VIII	1509–47
Edward VI	1547–53
Jane Grey	1553
Mary I	1553–58
Elizabeth I	1558–1603
James I	1603–25
Charles I	1625–49
Oliver Cromwell	1653–58
Richard Cromwell	1658–59
Charles II	1660–85
James II	1685–88
Mary II	1689–94*
William III	1689–1702*
Anne	1702–14
George I	1714–27
George II	1727–60
George III	1760–1820
George IV	1820–30
William IV	1830–37
Victoria	1837–1901
Edward VII	1901–10
George V	1910–36
Edward VIII	1936
George VI	1936–52
Elizabeth II	1952–

*Queen Mary II was the daughter of King James II. She reigned alongside her husband, William III, from 1689 until her death in 1694, at age thirty-two. William then reigned until 1702, when he died after falling from a horse and breaking his collarbone.

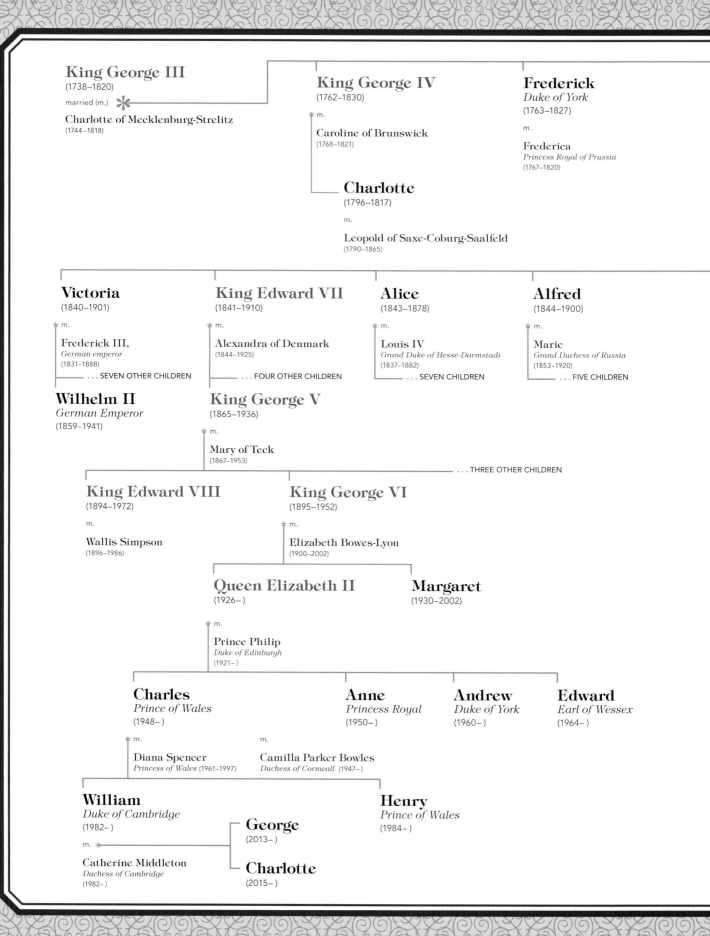

King George III
(1738–1820)

married (m.) ✳

Charlotte of Mecklenburg-Strelitz
(1744–1818)

King George IV
(1762–1830)

✳ m.

Caroline of Brunswick
(1768–1821)

Charlotte
(1796–1817)

m.

Leopold of Saxe-Coburg-Saalfeld
(1790–1865)

Frederick
Duke of York
(1763–1827)

m.

Frederica
Princess Royal of Prussia
(1767–1820)

Victoria
(1840–1901)

✳ m.

Frederick III,
German emperor
(1831–1888)
. . . SEVEN OTHER CHILDREN

Wilhelm II
German Emperor
(1859–1941)

King Edward VII
(1841–1910)

✳ m.

Alexandra of Denmark
(1844–1925)
. . . FOUR OTHER CHILDREN

King George V
(1865–1936)

✳ m.

Mary of Teck
(1867–1953)

Alice
(1843–1878)

✳ m.

Louis IV
Grand Duke of Hesse-Darmstadt
(1837–1882)
. . . SEVEN CHILDREN

Alfred
(1844–1900)

✳ m.

Marie
Grand Duchess of Russia
(1853–1920)
. . . FIVE CHILDREN

. . . THREE OTHER CHILDREN

King Edward VIII
(1894–1972)

m.

Wallis Simpson
(1896–1986)

King George VI
(1895–1952)

✳ m.

Elizabeth Bowes-Lyon
(1900–2002)

Queen Elizabeth II
(1926–)

✳ m.

Prince Philip
Duke of Edinburgh
(1921–)

Margaret
(1930–2002)

Charles
Prince of Wales
(1948–)

✳ m.

Diana Spencer
Princess of Wales (1961–1997)

m.

Camilla Parker Bowles
Duchess of Cornwall (1947–)

Anne
Princess Royal
(1950–)

Andrew
Duke of York
(1960–)

Edward
Earl of Wessex
(1964–)

William
Duke of Cambridge
(1982–)

m. ✳

Catherine Middleton
Duchess of Cambridge
(1982–)

George
(2013–)

Charlotte
(2015–)

Henry
Prince of Wales
(1984–)

King William IV
(1765–1837)

m.

Adelaide of Saxe-Meiningen
(1792–1849)

Edward
Duke of Kent
(1767–1820)

⁎ m.

Victoire of Saxe-Coburg-Saalfeld
(1786–1861)

♔
Queen Victoria
(1819–1901)

⁎ m.

Albert of Saxe-Coburg and Gotha
(1819–1861)

Helena
(1846–1923)

⁎ m.

Christian of
Schleswig-Holstein
(1831–1917)

└─ . . . FOUR CHILDREN

Louise
(1848–1939)

m.

John Campbell
Marquess of Lorne
(1845–1914)

Arthur
(1850–1942)

⁎ m.

Louise of Prussia
(1860–1917)

└─ . . . THREE CHILDREN

Leopold
(1853–1884)

⁎ m.

Helen of
Waldeck-Pyrmont
(1861–1922)

└─ . . . TWO CHILDREN

Beatrice
(1857–1944)

⁎ m.

Henry of Battenberg
(1858–1896)

└─ . . . FOUR CHILDREN

QUEEN VICTORIA'S
FAMILY TREE

NOTES

PROLOGUE: LONG LIVE THE QUEEN!

1 "for love or money": Mundy, *The Journal of Mary Frampton*, 405.

"The uproar, the confusion . . .": Greville, *The Greville Memoirs*, vol. 1, 105.

"a feeling that something awful . . .": Hibbert, *Queen Victoria*, 70.

3 "God save Queen Victoria! . . .": *A Diary of Royal Movements*, 98.

5 "On her dominions . . .": Tegg, *A Dictionary of Chronology*, 278.

9 "The vein of iron . . .": Wyndham, *Correspondence of Sarah Spencer*, 348.

"People were taken by surprise . . .": Reid, *Ask Sir James*, 33.

CHAPTER 1. ENGLAND'S HOPE

11 "She stood on high . . .": Hamilton, *A Record of the Life and Death*, 35.

"a sad and dire accident . . .": Boyd, *Life at Fonthill*, 234.

13 "My brothers are not so strong . . .": Duff, *Edward of Kent*, 268.

14 "as plump as a partridge . . .": Williams, *Becoming Queen Victoria*, 156.

"a model of strength . . .": Ibid., 157.

"Look at her well . . .": Longford, *Victoria R. I.*, 24.

17 "She drives me . . .": Williams, *Becoming Queen Victoria*, 173.

18 "When we were to begin . . .": and "She seems to be . . ." Argyll, *V.R.I.*, 57.

"The little Princess . . .": Ibid., 60.

19 "There! You see . . .": Longford, *Victoria R. I.*, 37.

"friendless and alone": Hibbert, *Queen Victoria*, 23.

21 "Nation's Hope": Hudson, *A Royal Conflict*, 56.

"not of so high a rank . . .": Ibid., 74.

23 "The men, women, children . . .": Esher, *The Girlhood of Queen Victoria*, vol. 1, 44–45.

"Can you be dead . . .": Hibbert, *Queen Victoria*, 39.

24   "beloved Lehzen . . .": Gill, *We Two*, 69.

"full of goodness . . .": Esher, *The Girlhood of Queen Victoria*, vol. 1, 157.

"very amiable": Hough, *Victoria and Albert*, 31.

"The more I see them . . .": *University Library of Autobiography*, vol. 14, 255.

25   "I cried bitterly . . .": Ibid., 256.

"a most unwarrantable liberty": Greville, *The Greville Memoirs*, vol. 2, 484.

27   "I trust in God . . .": Ibid., 485.

"For the future . . .": Ibid.

"very awkward, by God!": Hibbert, *Queen Victoria*, 47.

CHAPTER 2. REGINAMANIA

29   "in a very odd state": Hibbert, *Queen Victoria*, 50.

30   "poor stupid me": Woodham-Smith, vol. 1, 134.

"light & frivolous . . .": Hudson, *A Royal Conflict*, 128.

"the system of intimidation . . .": Gill, *We Two*, 73.

31   "Lord Conyngham then acquainted me . . .": Benson and Esher, *The Letters of Queen Victoria*, vol. 1, 97.

"Poor man . . .": Somerset, *The Life and Times of William IV*, 217.

34   "There never was anything . . .": Hibbert, *Queen Victoria*, 54.

"I place my firm reliance . . ." and "protect the rights . . .": *Annual Register*, 238.

"Her voice which is naturally beautiful . . .": Jennings, *The Croker Papers*, vol. 2, 359.

"with perfect calmness . . .": Greville, *The Greville Memoirs*, vol. 2, 519.

"had been his own daughter . . .": Ibid.

"I had to remind her . . .": Hibbert, *Queen Victoria*, 56.

35   "I am *Queen*": Benson and Esher, *The Letters of Queen Victoria*, vol. 1, 97.

36   "I am very young . . .": Ibid., 98.

"There are not *many* like him . . .": Mitchell, *Lord Melbourne*, 234.

37   "I never saw . . .": Ibid., 237.

38   "He knows about everybody . . .": Esher, *The Girlhood of Queen Victoria*, 305.

"a great thumping girl . . ." and "which made me laugh . . .": Wilson, *Victoria*, 84.

"Take care . . .": Williams, *Becoming Queen Victoria*, 307.

"His situation . . .": Jennings, *The Croker Papers*, vol. 2, 320.

39   "Whenever a question . . .": Benson and Esher, *The Letters of Queen Victoria*, vol. 1, 104.

"change the conversation . . .": Ibid., 80.

"Of the Queen . . .": "Chit-Chat About Art and Artists," 10.

40   "Reginamania": "Postscript," 9.

"This epidemic . . .": Ibid.

"really in person . . .": Williams, *Becoming Queen Victoria*, 292.

"Her size is below the middle . . .": Royall, "Queen Victoria as Seen by an American," 463.

"worry and torment": Hibbert, *Queen Victoria*, 61.

"sweet as a Virginia nightingale's": Royall, "Queen Victoria as Seen by an American," 463.

"A more homely little being . . .": Maxwell, *The Creevey Papers*, 668.

41   "a collection of stone pumpkins . . .": Smith, *George IV*, 137.

"so overloaded one upon another . . .": Lewis, *Extracts of the Journals and Correspondence*, vol. 2, 490.

CHAPTER 3. GROWING PAINS

43   "Kings, Priests, and Prophets": Eeles, *The English Coronation Service*, 107.

44   "Indeed, as far as we could judge . . .": "The Coronation," 5–6.

"scrambled with the eagerness of children . . .": *A Diary of Royal Movements*, vol. 1, 98.

"Mr. Alderman Harmer . . .": Ibid.

"You did it beautifully . . .": Benson and Esher, eds., *The Letters of Queen Victoria*, vol. 1, 159.

45   "We have no doubt . . .": Hibbert, *Queen Victoria in Her Letters and Journals*, 42.

"amazing spy . . .": Hibbert, *Queen Victoria*, 77.

48   "Although there is an enlargement . . .": "Sir James Clark's Statement," 243.

"great concern . . .": Hibbert, *Queen Victoria in Her Letters and Journals*, 42.

"was Her Majesty's own idea": "The Late Lady Flora Hastings," 2.

"wished to have hanged . . .": Charlot, *Victoria*, 136.

"such a nasty woman": Williams, *Becoming Queen Victoria*, 318.

49   "I felt *I* had done nothing . . .": Ibid., 323.

"If one of the purest . . .": *The Dangers of Evil Counsel*, 6.

"Living but for your duty . . .": Albert, *Queen Victoria's Sister*, 91–92.

51   "with honour to myself . . .": "Ministerial Manoeuvres," 762.

"with that firmness . . .": Benson and Esher, *The Letters of Queen Victoria*, vol. 1, 195.

"I really thought . . .": Mitchell, *Lord Melbourne*, 241.

51   "a poor helpless girl" and "The thought of ALL . . .": Hibbert, *Queen Victoria*, 92.

    "You must try . . .": Ibid., 93.

    "It is very hard . . .": Esher, *The Girlhood of Queen Victoria*, vol. 2, 162.

    "such a cold, odd man": Benson and Esher, *The Letters of Queen Victoria*, vol. 1, 200.

52   "I never saw . . .": and "He was quite perturbed": Ibid., 204.

    "They wish to treat me . . .": Wright, *The Strange History of Buckingham Palace*, 189.

    "She has made herself . . .": Williams, *Becoming Queen Victoria*, 321.

53   "How could they let the Queen . . .": Müller, *Memoirs of Baron Stockmar*, vol. 2, 13.

    "this half crazy . . .": Arthur Ponsonby, *Henry Ponsonby*, 206.

55   "So much for the *Oranges*": Hudson, *A Royal Conflict*, 116.

CHAPTER 4. TOO HAPPY!

57   "A young person like me . . .": Esher, *The Girlhood of Queen Victoria*, vol. 2, 192.

    "quite *going*": Hibbert, *Queen Victoria*, 107.

    "Dearest Albert took my face . . .": Wilson, *Victoria*, 96.

59   "would never have presumed . . .": Parker, *Sir Robert Peel from His Private Papers*, vol. 2, 414.

    "too happy": Hibbert, *Queen Victoria in Her Letters and Journals*, 57.

    "Victoria declared her love . . .": Williams, *Becoming Queen Victoria*, 333.

    "Albert's *beauty is most striking* . . .": Benson and Esher, *The Letters of Queen Victoria*, vol. 1, 237.

    "Oh! to feel I was, and am, loved . . .": Hibbert, *Queen Victoria in Her Letters and Journals*, 57.

    "Dearest, greatly beloved . . .": Jagow, *Letters of the Prince Consort*, 22–23.

60   "so nicely side by side . . .": Williams, *Becoming Queen Victoria*, 334.

    "All my thoughts . . .": Jagow, *Letters of the Prince Consort*, 26.

    "The room was full . . .": Rusk, *The Beautiful Life and Illustrious Reign of Queen Victoria*, 134.

    "Your Lordships will be seated": Jennings, *The Croker Papers*, vol. 2, 359.

62   "It is my intention . . .": Charles Greville, untitled notice in the *Times*, November 25, 1839, p. 4.

    "Her hands trembled . . .": Greville, *The Greville Memoirs*, vol. 1, 247.

    "I felt my hands shook . . .": Rusk, *The Beautiful Life and Illustrious Reign of Queen Victoria*, 134.

63   "I felt most happy . . .": Ibid.

    "Were Prince Albert . . .": Untitled editorial in the *Times*, February 10, 1840, p. 4.

    "He comes to take . . .": St. Aubyn, *Queen Victoria*, 133.

    "Do what one will . . .": Hibbert, *Queen Victoria*, 113.

64　"We have Coburgs enough": Ziegler, *Melbourne*, 254.

　　"It is MY marriage . . .": St. Aubyn, *Queen Victoria*, 142.

　　"I never remember having suffered . . .": Jagow, *Letters of the Prince* Consort, 60.

　　"Seeing his *dear dear* face . . .": Plowden, *The Young Victoria*, 247.

65　"everything was always made . . .": Williams, *Becoming Queen Victoria*, 344.

66　"The low houses are all huddled . . .": Untitled editorial in the *Poor Man's Guardian*, February 18, 1832, p. 282.

67　"Those who are poor . . .": Mitchell, *Lord Melbourne*, 27.

　　"I don't like these things . . .": Ibid.

68　"Many of them excited roars . . .": "Celebration of Her Majesty's Marriage with His Royal Highness Prince Albert of Saxe Coburg and Gotha," 4.

69　"every known colour": Ibid.

　　"Every sympathy was awakened . . .": Ibid., 5.

　　"looked like village girls . . .": Wyndham, *Correspondence of Sarah Spencer*, 298.

　　"We were all huddled together . . .": Argyll, *V.R.I.*, 120.

　　"The Queen's look . . .": Wyndham, *Correspondence of Sarah Spencer*, 298.

72　"Ill or not . . .": Wilson, *Victoria*, 103.

CHAPTER 5. PRINCE VERSUS QUEEN

73　"at least a fortnight . . .": Weintraub, *Uncrowned King*, 95.

　　"You forget, my dearest Love . . .": Benson and Esher, *The Letters of Queen Victoria*, vol. 1, 269.

　　"I am only the husband . . .": Jagow, *Letters of the Prince Consort*, 69.

74　"The English are very jealous . . .": Benson and Esher, *The Letters of Queen Victoria*, vol. 1, 252.

　　"warped in many respects . . .": Hibbert, *Queen Victoria*, 126.

　　"I prayed God night and day . . .": Williams, *Becoming Queen Victoria*, 352.

76　"the benevolent and persevering exertions . . .": "First Anniversary Meeting of the Society for the Extinction of the Slave Trade," 6.

　　"small, disagreeable looking man": Bolitho, *The Prince Consort and His Brother*, 19.

　　"If it please Providence . . .": Mullen and Munson, *Victoria*, 93.

77　"long and loud huzzahs": "Atrocious Attempt to Assassinate the Queen and Prince Albert," 4.

　　"now all the fashion . . .": Hibbert, *Queen Victoria*, 131.

　　"I have my hands very full": Bolitho, *The Prince Consort and His Brother*, 34.

79   "the natural head . . .": Hibbert, *Queen Victoria*, 134.

"I am wonderfully well . . .": Charlot, *Victoria*, 195.

"was like that of a mother . . .": Williams, *Becoming Queen Victoria*, 358.

80   "She has big dark blue eyes . . .": Charlot, *Victoria*, 195.

Eleven days was the *longest* . . .": Benson and Esher, *The Letters of Queen Victoria*, vol. 1, 402.

"The Prince understands everything . . .": Hibbert, *Queen Victoria*, 135.

"She would like him better . . .": Greville, *The Greville Memoirs*, vol. 2, 44.

"first and greatest duty . . .": and "Perfectly": Ibid., 38.

"In short, he was more than satisfied . . .": Ibid.

82   "when one is so happy . . .": Hibbert, *Queen Victoria*, 137.

"one universal feeling of joy . . .": Untitled editorial in the *Times*, November 10, 1841, p. 4.

84   "There can be no improvement . . .": Hibbert, *Queen Victoria*, 152.

"She will not hear me out . . .": James, *Albert, Prince Consort*, 127.

85   "Take the child away . . .": Ibid., 126.

"Albert must tell me . . ." and "When I am in a passion . . .": Charlot, *Victoria*, 211.

"There is often an irritability . . .": James, *Albert, Prince Consort*, 128.

"It was very painful . . .": Wyndham, *Correspondence of Sarah Spencer*, 331.

86   "No bird can return . . .": Margetson, *Victorian High Society*, 136.

"over-watched and over-doctored": Wyndham, *Correspondence of Sarah Spencer*, 322.

Lyttelton, "garter-blue velvet . . .": Ibid., 334.

87   "Nothing could go on better . . .": Charlot, *Victoria*, 218.

CHAPTER 6. FAMILY LIFE

89   "agitated": Wilson, *Victoria*, 207.

"the sailor-gypsy life": Hibbert, *Queen Victoria*, 166.

90   "They whole family received us with a heartiness . . .": Martin, *The Life of His Royal Highness the Prince Consort*, vol. 1, 181.

"as amused as a child . . .": Surtees, *Charlotte Canning*, 97.

91   "very merry and laughed . . .": Hibbert, *Queen Victoria*, 167.

92   "I feel so gay and happy . . .": St. Aubyn, *Queen Victoria*, 239.

"Somehow it was not pretty . . .": Surtees, *Charlotte Canning*, 101.

"decidedly very badly chosen . . .": Ibid., 110.

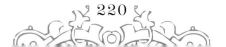

92 "would do for an old woman . . .": Ibid., 115.

"The stay was *so delightful* . . .": Benson and Esher, *The Letters of Queen Victoria*, vol. 1, 615–16.

93 "strange Chinese thing . . .": Charlot, *Victoria*, 283.

"all that is grand . . .": Vectis, *The Isle of Wight Tourist*, 5.

"It is impossible . . .": Hibbert, *Queen Victoria*, 162.

"I, partly forester . . .": Martin, *The Life of His Royal Highness the Prince Consort*, vol. 1, 322–23.

96 "She there enjoys her domestic life . . .": Bunsen, *A Memoir of Baron Bunsen*, vol. 2, 229.

98 "not very nice": Fulford, *Dearest Child*, 195.

"He is so kind . . .": James, *Albert, Prince Consort*, 231.

"They say, no Sovereign . . .": Martin, *The Life of His Royal Highness the Prince Consort*, vol. 1, 243.

100 "Hungry in a land of plenty . . .": "The Autobiography of One of the Chartist Rebels of 1848," 383.

101 "European war . . .": Martin, *The Life of His Royal Highness the Prince Consort*, vol. 1, 480.

"to the credit . . .": Browne, *Wellington*, 295.

"No Cheese," "Pugnose," "Mr Punch": Postgate, *Revolution from 1789 to 1906*, 111.

102 "I never was calmer . . .": Martin, *The Life of His Royal Highness the Prince Consort*, vol. 1, 481.

103 "wanton & worthless men": Hibbert, *Queen Victoria*, 203.

"They seldom lose the hand . . .": Children's Employment Commission, *Second Report of the Commissioners*, 90–91.

104 "most of the toil . . .": *The Principal Speeches and Addresses*, 88–89.

105 "Truly & sincerely . . .": Martin, *The Life of His Royal Highness the Prince Consort*, vol. 2, 156–57.

CHAPTER 7. THE MODERN WORLD

109 "by encouraging the arts . . .": "The Opening of the Great Exhibition," 4.

"The exhibition has taught me . . .": Fay, *Palace of Industry*, 67.

"one of the greatest . . .": Ibid., 46.

"It gives me a pang . . ." Hibbert, *Queen Victoria*, 399.

110 "lowness and tendency to cry . . .": Fulford, *Dearest Child*, 162.

111 "I am often astonished . . .": Hibbert, *Queen Victoria*, 218.

"a pretty little castle . . .": Victoria, Queen of Great Britain, *Leaves from the Journal of Our Life in the Highlands*, 101.

"my dearest Albert's *own* creation . . .": Ibid., 158.

"All seemed to breathe freedom . . .": Ibid., 102.

111 "clear as glass": Ibid., 50.

"delightfully soft to walk upon": Ibid., 55.

"Scotch air, Scotch people . . .": Wyndham, *Correspondence of Sarah Spencer*, 393.

114 "There are few English boys . . .": Hibbert, *Queen Victoria*, 188.

115 "I seem to have got at his heart . . .": Charlot, *Victoria*, 296.

"It has been a terrible sorrow . . .": *H.R.H. The Prince of Wales*, 10–11.

116 "an exaggerated Copy . . .": "The Education of a Prince," 110.

117 "beloved troops": Hibbert, *Queen Victoria*, 224.

"You never saw anyone . . .": Carlton, *Royal Warriors*, 146.

118 "I envy her . . .": Ibid.

119 "such fine, powerful frames . . .": Hibbert, *Queen Victoria*, 223–24.

"God bless our Queen": "The Queen's Visit to the Wounded Soldiers."

120 "possessed of *indomitable courage* . . .": Benson and Esher, *The Letters of Queen Victoria*, vol. 3, 122.

121 "charming lovable creature" and "lively & talkative": Hibbert, *Queen Victoria*, 233.

CHAPTER 8. "OH, THIS IS DEATH"

123 "she had on a massive bonnet . . .": Munich, *Queen Victoria's Secrets*, 67.

125 "I was thought so dignified . . .": Stoney and Weltzein, eds. *My Mistress the Queen*, 17.

"I should like to be . . .": Hibbert, *Queen Victoria*, 237.

126 "for *one* of the happiest days . . .": Ibid., 238.

127 "I felt as if I were being married . . .": Argyll, *V.R.I.*, 248.

"darling flower": Ibid., 249.

"so lost without Vicky": Martin, *The Life of His Royal Highness the Prince Consort*, vol. 4, 163.

"an innocent girl . . .": Wilson, *Victoria*, 210.

129 "the horrors committed in India . . .": Ibid., 213.

130 "*day* and night": Hibbert, *Queen Victoria*, 249.

131 "that there is no hatred . . .": Ibid., 250.

"feelings of generosity . . .": Ibid., 251.

"I shall never see . . .": Ibid., 262.

132 "Such a little love!" Ibid., 261.

"tears were trickling down . . .": Weintraub, *Uncrowned King*, 394.

"It is *dreadful* . . .": Hibbert, *Queen Victoria*, 266.

132   "*She* is gone . . .": Benson and Esher, *The Letters of Queen Victoria*, vol. 3, 435.

"I do not wish . . .": Fulford, *Dearest Child*, 319.

"Such touching relics . . .": Ashdown, *Queen Victoria's Mother*, 147.

134   "as if it was . . .": Kennedy, *My Dear Duchess*, 141.

"cried when I kissed him . . .": Fulford, *Dearest Child*, 362.

135   "It would be a thousand pities . . .": Hibbert, *Queen Victoria*, 273.

"charming and very pretty": Hibbert, *Edward VII*, 45.

136   "many infinitely worse cases": Wilson, *Victoria*, 254.

"The malady is very grave . . .": Hough, *Victoria and Albert*, 190.

"I prayed & cried . . .": Ibid., 191.

"Oh, this is death": Wilson, *Victoria*, 255.

"Oh my dear Darling": Ibid.

"pretty, winning ways . . .": Cartwright, *The Journals of Lady Knightley of Fawsley*, 31.

137   "Poor Mama is more wretched . . .": Zeepvat, *Prince Leopold*, 32.

CHAPTER 9. WHERE IS QUEEN VICTORIA?

141   "What he has done . . .": Vicinus and Nergaard, *Ever Yours, Florence Nightingale*, 232.

"We have lost a great and good prince . . .": Rappaport, *A Magnificent Obsession*, 89.

"Him whom she loved . . .": "Albert," 245.

142   "it is expected . . .": Rappaport, *A Magnificent Obsession*, 95.

143   "Oh! how I admired Papa . . .": Fulford, *Dearest Mama*, 24.

"A Voice told me . . .": Cullen, *The Empress Brown*, 60.

144   "that blessed guardian angel . . .": St. Aubyn, *Edward VII*, 79.

"*He* gives you his blessing!" Hibbert, *Queen Victoria*, 303.

146   "Isn't it better . . .": Ibid., 308.

"very stout, very red . . .": Hudson, *Munby: Man of Two Worlds*, 218.

"I felt as if I should faint . . .": Hibbert, *Queen Victoria*, 312.

147   "climbed to the top . . .": Fraser, *Disraeli and His Day*, 52.

148   "Everyone likes flattery . . .": Buckle, *The Life of Benjamin Disraeli*, 463.

"an advantage in judgement . . .": Hibbert, *Queen Victoria*, 317.

"Is that so?": Benson, *As We Were*, 96.

"He will not attend . . .": Ibid., 95.

149 "the People's William": Wilson, *Victoria*, 139.

150 "severe Highland scenery . . .": Victoria, Queen of Great Britain, *Leaves from the Journal of Our Life in the Highlands*, 113, 136.

"the Queen's Highland Servant": Gill, *We Two*, 379.

"You've said enough": Longford, *Victoria R. I.*, 459.

"Masters and mistresses . . .": Baylis, *The Rights, Duties, and Relations*, 26.

151 "selected this man . . .": Vincent, *Disraeli, Derby, and the Conservative Party*, 247–48.

"a real treasure": Hibbert, *Queen Victoria in Her Letters and Journals*, 188.

"I have here always . . .": Hibbert, *Queen Victoria*, 325.

"He alone talks to her . . .": Cullen, *The Empress Brown*, 131.

"I won't have an absurd man . . .": Ibid., 123.

154 "*for Louise's happiness* . . .": Buckle, *The Letters of Queen Victoria*, vol. 1, 632.

"This frightful bloodshed . . .": Lucinda Hawksley, *Queen Victoria's Mysterious Daughter*, 118.

"A feeling of satisfaction . . .": Ibid., 126.

"daughter of the horse-leech . . .": "A Working Man," "English Republicanism," 755.

156 "They regard Prince Arthur . . .": "The Cost of Royalty," 3.

"Is there no sort of labour . . .": Ibid.

"Her Majesty has done much . . .": "Continued Opposition to the Dowry of the Princess Louise," 3.

CHAPTER 10. A TALE OF TWO PRIME MINISTERS

157 "Throughout India . . .": *A Reprint from the Times*, 468.

"Really the way in which they all squabble . . .": Battiscombe, *Queen Alexandra*, 116–17.

158 "I hardly knew how . . .": Hibbert, *Queen Victoria*, 343.

"Oh! dear Mama . . .": Ibid., 344.

"gentler and kinder . . .": Ibid.

"From the highest . . .": Wilson, *Victoria*, 351.

"had a smile . . .": "The National Thanksgiving Day."

"It was, of course . . .": Wilson, *Victoria*, 351.

159 "a great holyday . . .": "The National Thanksgiving Day."

160 "all Foreign Potentates . . .": Weintraub, *Victoria*, 354.

"uncivilized": Hibbert, *Queen Victoria*, 347.

"fairly tall and not fat . . .": Wright, *The Persians Among the English*, 129.

160   "There was nothing . . .": Ibid.

163   "His mind and head . . .": Fulford, *Your Dear Letter*, 184.

      "You fancy you are stronger . . .": Zeepvat, *Prince Leopold*, 77.

      "full of poetry . . .": Collier and Marriott, *Colonisation and Conflict,* 98.

      "She is the metropolis . . .": Lee, *Gladstone and Disraeli*, 30.

166   "so much better for their being wild": Buckle, *The Life of Benjamin Disraeli*, vol. 6, 628.

      "There was not a house . . .": MacGahan, "The Turkish Atrocities in Bulgaria."

167   "I entreat my countrymen . . .": Gladstone, *Bulgarian Horrors and the Question of the East*, 31.

      "half madman . . .": Leonard, *The Great Rivalry*, 169.

      "unprincipled maniac . . .": Ibid., 168.

169   "[It had] aged and shaken . . .": Wilson, *Victoria*, 391.

      "It was a sad birthday . . .": Ibid.

      "a lesson *never* to reduce . . .": Buckle, *The Life of Benjamin Disraeli*, vol. 6, 464.

      "The foreign policy . . .": Handcock, *English Historical Documents,* 361.

170   "The sanctity of life . . .": Smith, *The Life of the Right Honourable William Ewart Gladstone*, vol. 5, 23.

171   "the kindest and most devoted . . .": Hibbert, *Queen Victoria*, 368.

      "who would soon ruin . . .": Jenkins, *Gladstone*, 270.

      "There must be no democratic leaning . . .": Handcock, *English Historical Documents*, 28.

      "a bitter trial . . .": Fulford, *Beloved Mama*, 75.

      "I can scarcely see . . .": Wilson, *Victoria*, 402.

173   "his strength of will . . .": Buckle, *The Life of Benjamin Disraeli*, vol. 6, 622.

CHAPTER 11. "THE QUEEN IS ENOUGH TO KILL ANYONE"

175   "very miserable": Hibbert, *Queen Victoria*, 441.

      "I have lost my dearest best friend . . .": Cullen, *The Empress Brown*, 225.

      "The shock—the blow . . .": Weintraub, *Victoria*, 391.

176   "We can feel for her . . .": Zeepvat, *Prince Leopold*, 177.

      "a most absurd fancy . . .": Wilson, *Victoria*, 428.

177   "I feel I should be wanting . . .": Ibid., 429.

      "How dear he was to me . . .": Hibbert, *Queen Victoria in Her Letters and Journals*, 285.

179   "struggling rightly to be free": Richard Shannon, *Gladstone*, vol. 2, 332.

      "The Queen trembles . . .": Frank Hardie, *The Political Influence of Queen Victoria*, 83.

180   "To think that all this might have been prevented . . .": Buckle, ed., *The Letters of Queen Victoria*, vol. 3, 597.

"The Queen is enough . . .": Tom Crewe, "Disraeli's Flowery History."

"He will be for ever branded . . .": Fulford, *Beloved Mama*, 183. St. John, *Gladstone and the Logic of Victorian Politics*, 289.

181   "when once he had convinced . . .": Benson, *As We Were*, 94–95.

"I cannot help . . .": Hibbert, *Queen Victoria*, 374.

"Grand Old Man": Wilson, *Victoria*, 397.

182   "one of the most intelligent . . .": Ramm, *Beloved and Darling Child*, 28.

"She had an extraordinary knowledge . . .": Hardie, *The Political Influence of Queen Victoria*, 246.

"distinguished merit . . .": "Albert Medal," 751.

"the personal embodiment . . .": Ibid., 752.

183   "Now, Mother . . .": *The Private Life of Queen Victoria*, 68.

"After the jewels . . .": Benson, *As We Were*, 105.

184   "great pain . . .": Wilson, *Victoria*, 464.

186   "zealous, attentive . . .": Basu, *Victoria and Abdul*, 70.

"the poor Munshi's sensitive feelings": Hibbert, *Queen Victoria*, 449.

"She really likes the emotional excitement . . .": Nelson, *Queen Victoria and the Discovery of the Riviera*, 123.

191   "It was Queen Victoria": Olson, *Harold Nicolson*, 224.

"I never saw two people . . .": Milner, *My Picture Gallery*, 230.

"the warmest and closest . . .": Cecil, *Life of Robert, Marquis of Salisbury*, vol. 3, 192.

CHAPTER 12. THE LAST PROCESSION

193   "These are trying moments": Hibbert, *Queen Victoria*, 374.

"an old, wild, incomprehensible man . . .": Ibid., 375.

"Hats were knocked off . . .": Luce, *A Diary of the Home Rule Parliament*, 201.

195   "He was a great Englishman . . .": Ramm, *Beloved and Darling Child*, 215.

"He was a clever man . . .": Ibid.

"It is not possible . . .": Carnegie, "Some Important Results of the Jubilee," 506.

"She followed the life . . .": Wells, *Experiment in Autobiography*, vol. 1, 46.

196   "The little black figure . . .": Benson, *As We Were*, 106.

       "It seems to me . . .": Hibbert, *Queen Victoria*, 415.

197   "Please understand . . .": Farwell, *The Great Boer War*, 142.

200   "this dear, excellent, gallant boy . . .": Hibbert, *Queen Victoria*, 487.

       "When she breaks down . . .": Mallet, *Life with Queen Victoria*, 212.

       "After the Prince Consort's death . . .": Ibid., 213.

201   "and now we are in the Twentieth Century . . .": Bell, *Randall Davidson*, 353–54.

       "She reigned by sheer force of character . . .": Larned, *History for Ready Reference*, 213–14.

203   "great and wise Father": *London Gazette Extraordinary*, January 23, 1901.

       "the Queen! The Queen!" Rennell, *Last Days of Glory*, 262.

205   "has ceased to believe . . .": Craik, *Fifty Golden Years*, 63.

       "She had kindled the imagination . . .": Benson, *As We Were*, 106.

BIBLIOGRAPHY

"Albert." *Punch*, December 21, 1861, p. 245.

Albert, Harold A. *Queen Victoria's Sister: The Life and Letters of Princess Feodora*. London: Robert Hale, 1967.

"Albert Medal." *Journal of the Society of Arts*, June 10, 1887, pp. 751–52.

The Annual Register, or a View of the History, Politics, and Literature, of the Year 1837. London: Baldwin and Cradock, 1838.

"Atrocious Attempt to Assassinate the Queen and Prince Albert." *London Times*, June 11, 1840, 4.

Argyll, John Douglas. *V.R.I.: Her Life and Empire*. New York: Harper and Brothers, 1901.

Ashdown, Dulcie M. *Queen Victoria's Mother*. London: Robert Hale, 1974.

"The Autobiography of One of the Chartist Rebels of 1848." *Christian Socialist*, December 13, 1851, pp. 381–83.

Basu, Shrabani. *Victoria and Abdul: The True Story of the Queen's Closest Confidant*. Stroud, Gloucestershire, U.K.: History Press, 2010.

Battiscombe, Georgina. *Queen Alexandra*. London: Constable, 1969.

Baylis, T. Henry. *The Rights, Duties, and Relations of Domestic Servants, Their Masters and Mistresses*. London: Sampson Low, Son, and Co., 1857.

Bell, G. K. A. *Randall Davidson: Archbishop of Canterbury*. London: Geoffrey Cumberlege, 1952.

Benson, Arthur Christopher, and Reginald Baliol Brett Esher, eds. *The Letters of Queen Victoria: A Selection from Her Majesty's Correspondence Between the Years 1837 and 1861*. 3 vols. New York: Longmans, Green and Co., 1907–8.

Benson, E. F. *As We Were: A Victorian Peep Show*. London: Longmans, Green and Co., 1930.

Black's Picturesque Tourist of Scotland. Edinburgh: Adam and Charles Black, 1850.

Bolitho, Hector, ed. *The Prince Consort and His Brother: Two Hundred New Letters*. New York: D. Appleton-Century Company, 1934.

Boyd, Alexander, ed. *Life at Fonthill, 1807–1822, with Interludes in Paris and London*. London: Rupert Hart Davis, 1957.

Browne, G. Lathom. *Wellington: Or, the Public and Private Life of Arthur, First Duke of Wellington*. London: W. H. Allen and Company, 1888.

Buckle, George Earle. *The Life of Benjamin Disraeli, Earl of Beaconsfield*. Vol. 6: *1876–1881*. New York, Macmillan, 1920.

———. ed. *The Letters of Queen Victoria*. 3 vols. London: John Murray, 1926–28.

Bunsen, Frances Waddington. *A Memoir of Baron Bunsen*. Vol. 2. London: Longmans, Green, and Co., 1868.

Carlton, Charles. *Royal Warriors: A Military History of the British Monarchy*. London: Routledge, 2014.

Carnegie, Andrew. "Some Important Results of the Jubilee." *North American Review*, October 1897, pp. 497–506.

Cartwright, Julia, ed. *The Journals of Lady Knightley of Fawsley, 1856–1884*. New York: E. P. Dutton and Co., 1917.

Cecil, Gwendolen. *Life of Robert, Marquis of Salisbury*. Vol. 3: *1880–1886*. London: Hodder and Stoughton, 1931.

"Celebration of Her Majesty's Marriage with His Royal Highness Prince Albert of Saxe Coburg and Gotha. *Times*, February 11, 1840, pp. 4–6.

Charlot, Monica. *Victoria: The Young Queen*. Oxford: Blackwell, 1991.

Children's Employment Commission. *Second Report of the Commissioners: Trades and Manufactures*. London: William Clowes and Sons, 1843.

"Chit-Chat About Art and Artists." *Art-Union*, February 1839, p. 10.

Collier, Martin, and Bill Marriott. *Colonisation and Conflict, 1750–1990*. Oxford: Heinemann, 2002.

"Continued Opposition to the Dowry of the Princess Louise." *Perth Gazette and West Australian Times*, May 12, 1871, p. 3.

"The Coronation." *Times*, June 29, 1838, pp. 2–6.

"The Cost of Royalty." *Pall Mall Budget*, July 21, 1871, 3.

Craik, Mrs. *Fifty Golden Years: Incidents in the Queen's Reign*. Swindon, U.K.: English Heritage, 2006.

Crewe, Tom. "Disraeli's Flowery Legacy." Government of the United Kingdom. Available online: history.blog.gov.uk/2013/04/29/disraelis-flowery-history; accessed on May 8, 2016.

Cullen, Tom. *The Empress Brown: The True Story of a Victorian Scandal*. Boston: Houghton Mifflin, 1969.

✦ BIBLIOGRAPHY ✦

The Dangers of Evil Counsel: A Voice from the Grave of Lady Flora Hastings. 2nd ed. London: T. Cadell, 1839.

A Diary of Royal Movements and of Personal Events and Incidents in the Life and Reign of Her Most Gracious Majesty Queen Victoria. Vol. 1. London: Elliot Stock, 1883.

Duff, David. *Edward of Kent: The Story of Queen Victoria's Father.* London: Muller, 1973.

"The Education of a Prince: Extracts from the Diaries of Frederick Weymouth Gibbs, 1851–1856." *Cornhill Magazine*, spring 1951, pp. 104–19.

Eeles, F. C. *The English Coronation Service: Its History and Teaching.* Oxford: A. R. Mowbray and Co., 1902.

Esher, Reginald Baliol Brett, ed. *The Girlhood of Queen Victoria.* 2 vols. New York: Longmans, Green and Co., 1912.

Farwell, Byron. *The Great Boer War.* London: Allen Lane, 1977.

Fay, C. R. *Palace of Industry, 1851: A Study of the Great Exhibition and Its Fruits.* Cambridge: Cambridge University Press, 1951.

"First Anniversary Meeting of the Society for the Extinction of the Slave Trade and for the Civilization of Africa." *Times*, June 2, 1840, pp. 6–7.

Fraser, William. *Disraeli and His Day.* London: Kegan Paul, Trench, Trübner and Co., 1891.

Fulford, Roger, ed. *Beloved Mama: Private Correspondence of Queen Victoria and the German Crown Princess, 1878–1885.* London: Evans Brothers, 1981.

———. *Dearest Child: Letters Between Queen Victoria and the Princess Royal, 1858–1861.* London: Evans Brothers, 1964.

———. *Dearest Mama: Letters Between Queen Victoria and the Crown Princess of Prussia, 1861–1864.* London: Evans Brothers, 1968.

———. *Your Dear Letter: Private Correspondence of Queen Victoria and the Crown Princess of Prussia, 1865–1871.* London: Evans Brothers, 1971.

Gill, Gillian. *We Two: Victoria and Albert.* New York: Ballantine, 2009.

Gladstone, W. E. *Bulgarian Horrors and the Question of the East.* London: John Murray, 1876.

Greville, Charles C. F. *The Greville Memoirs: A Journal of the Reigns of King George IV and King William IV.* Vol. 2. New York: D. Appleton and Company, 1883.

———. *The Greville Memoirs: A Journal of the Reign of Queen Victoria from 1837 to 1852.* Vol. 1. London: Longmans, Green, and Co., 1885.

H.R.H. The Prince of Wales. London: Grant Richards, 1898.

Hamilton, Edwin B. *A Record of the Life and Death of Her Royal Highness the Princess Charlotte.* London: J. Bumpus, 1817.

Handcock, W. D., ed. *English Historical Documents, 1874–1914.* London: Routledge, 2000.

Hardie, Frank. *The Political Influence of Queen Victoria, 1861–1901.* London: Oxford University Press, 1935.

Hawksley, Lucinda. *Queen Victoria's Mysterious Daughter: A Biography of Princess Louise.* New York: Thomas Dunne, 2015.

Hibbert, Christopher. *Edward VII: A Portrait.* London: Allen Lane, 1976.

———. *Queen Victoria: A Personal History.* Cambridge, Mass.: Da Capo Press, 2000.

———. *Queen Victoria in Her Letters and Journals.* London: John Murray, 1984.

Hough, Richard. *Victoria and Albert.* New York: St. Martin's Press, 1996.

Hudson, Derek. *Munby: Man of Two Worlds.* London: John Murray, 1972.

Hudson, Katherine. *A Royal Conflict: Sir John Conroy and the Young Victoria.* London: John Curtis, 1994.

Jagow, Kurt, ed. *Letters of the Prince Consort, 1831–1861.* London: John Murray, 1938.

James, Robert Rhodes. *Albert, Prince Consort: A Biography.* London: Hamish Hamilton, 1983.

Jenkins, Roy. *Gladstone: A Biography.* New York: Random House, 1997.

Jennings, Louis J., ed. *The Croker Papers: The Correspondence and Diaries of the Late Right Honourable John Wilson Croker, LL.D., F.R.S.* Vol. 2. London: John Murray, 1884.

Kennedy, A. L., ed. *My Dear Duchess: Social and Political Letters to the Duchess of Manchester, 1858–1869.* London: John Murray, 1956.

Larned, J. N. *History for Ready Reference.* Springfield, Mass.: C. A. Nichols Co., 1901.

"The Late Lady Flora Hastings." *London Morning Post.* September 14, 1839, pp. 2–3.

Lee, Stephen J. *Gladstone and Disraeli.* London: Routledge, 2005.

Leonard, Dick. *The Great Rivalry: Gladstone & Disraeli.* London: I. B. Taurus, 2013.

Lewis, Lady Theresa, ed. *Extracts of the Journals and Correspondence of Miss Berry from the Year 1783 to 1852.* Vol. 2. London: Longmans, Green and Co., 1865.

Longford, Elizabeth. *Victoria R. I.* London: Weidenfeld and Nicolson, 1964.

Luce, Henry W. *A Diary of the Home Rule Parliament, 1892–1895.* London: Cassell and Co., 1896.

MacGahan, J. A. "The Turkish Atrocities in Bulgaria: Horrible Scenes at Batak." *London Daily News,* August 22, 1876.

✦ BIBLIOGRAPHY ✦

Mallet, Victor, ed., *Life with Queen Victoria: Marie Mallet's Letters from Court, 1887–1901*. Boston: Houghton Mifflin, 1968.

Margetson, Stella. *Victorian High Society*. New York: Holmes and Meier, 1980.

Martin, Theodore. *The Life of His Royal Highness the Prince Consort*. 5 vols. London: Smith, Elder and Co., 1875–76.

Maxwell, Herbert, ed. *The Creevey Papers: A Selection from the Correspondence and Diaries of the Late Thomas Creevey, M.P.* New York: E. P. Dutton and Company, 1904.

McClintock, Mary Howard. *The Queen Thanks Sir Howard: The Life of Major-General Sir Howard Elphinstone, V. C., K. C. B., C. M. G.* London: John Murray, 1945.

Milner, Violet Georgina. *My Picture Gallery, 1886–1901*. London: John Murray, 1951.

"Ministerial Manoeuvres." *Dublin University Magazine*, June 1839, pp. 757–63.

Mitchell, L. G. *Lord Melbourne, 1779–1848*. Oxford: Oxford University Press, 1997.

Mullen, Richard, and James Munson. *Victoria: Portrait of a Queen*. London: BBC Books, 1987.

Müller, Max, ed. *Memoirs of Baron Stockmar by His Son Baron E. von Stockmar*. Vol. 2. London: Longmans, Green and Co., 1873.

Mundy, Harriot Georgiana, ed. *The Journal of Mary Frampton, from the Year 1779, Until the Year 1846*. London: Sampson Low, Marston, Searle, and Rivington, 1885.

Munich, Adrienne. *Queen Victoria's Secrets*. New York: Columbia University Press, 1996.

"The National Thanksgiving Day." *Times*, February 28, 1872.

Nelson, Michael. *Queen Victoria and the Discovery of the Riviera*. London: Tauris Parke, 2007.

Olson, Stanley, ed. *Harold Nicolson: Diaries and Letters, 1930–1964*. London: Collins, 1980.

"The Opening of the Great Exhibition." *Times*, May 2, 1851, 4.

Parker, Charles Stuart, ed. *Sir Robert Peel from His Private Papers*. Vol. 2. London: John Murray, 1899.

Plowden, Alison. *The Young Victoria*. Stroud, Gloucestershire, U.K.: History Press, 2010.

Ponsonby, Arthur. *Henry Ponsonby: Queen Victoria's Private Secretary*. New York: Macmillan, 1943.

Postgate, R. W. *Revolution from 1789 to 1906*. Boston: Houghton Mifflin, 1888.

"Postscript." *Spectator*, January 6, 1838, p. 9.

The Principal Speeches and Addresses of His Royal Highness the Prince Consort. London: John Murray, 1862.

The Private Life of Queen Victoria by One of Her Majesty's Servants. London: C. Arthur Pearson, 1901.

"The Queen's Visit to the Wounded Soldiers at Fort Pitt and Brompton." *Cornwall Chronicle*, July 20, 1855.

Ramm, Agatha, ed., *Beloved and Darling Child: Last Letters Between Queen Victoria and Her Eldest Daughter, 1886–1901*. Far Thrupp, Stroud, Gloucestershire, U.K.: Alan Sutton, 1990.

Rappaport, Helen. *A Magnificent Obsession: Victoria, Albert, and the Death That Changed the British Monarchy*. New York: St. Martin's Press, 2011.

Reid, Michaela. *Ask Sir James: Sir James Reid, Personal Physician to Queen Victoria*. New York: Penguin Books, 1987.

Rennell, Tony. *Last Days of Glory: The Death of Queen Victoria*. London: Viking, 2000.

A Reprint from the Times: The Annual Summaries for a Quarter of a Century. London: Times Office, 1876.

Royall, William, arr. "Queen Victoria as Seen by an American." *Century Illustrated Monthly Magazine*, November 1908–April 1909, pp. 453–63.

Rusk, John. *The Beautiful Life and Illustrious Reign of Queen Victoria*. Lansing, Mich.: P. A. Stone and Co., 1901.

Shannon, Richard. *Gladstone*. Vol. 2: *1865–1898*. Chapel Hill: University of North Carolina Press, 1999.

"Sir James Clark's Statement of the Case of the Late Lady Flora Hastings." *American Journal of the Medical Sciences*. Philadelphia: Lea and Blanchard, 1839, pp. 241–44.

Smith, E. A. *George IV*. New Haven: Yale University Press, 1999.

Smith, George Barnett. *The Life of the Right Honourable William Ewart Gladstone*. London: Cassell, Petter, Galpin and Co., n.d.

Somerset, Anne. *The Life and Times of William IV*. London: Weidenfeld and Nicolson, 1980.

St. Aubyn, Giles. *Edward VII: Prince and King*. New York: Atheneum, 1979.

———. *Queen Victoria*. New York: Atheneum, 1992.

St. John, Ian. *Gladstone and the Logic of Victorian Politics*. London: Anthem Press, 2010.

Stoney, Benita, and Heinrich C. Weltzein, eds. *My Mistress the Queen: The Letters of Frieda Arnold, Dresser to Queen Victoria, 1854–9*. London: Weidenfeld and Nicholson, 1994.

Surtees, Virginia. *Charlotte Canning: Lady-in-Waiting to Queen Victoria and Wife of the First Viceroy of India*. London: John Murray, 1975.

Tegg, Thomas. *A Dictionary of Chronology*. London: Thomas Tegg and Son, 1835.

University Library of Autobiography. Vol. 14. New York: F. Tyler Daniels Company, 1918.

Vectis, Philo. *The Isle of Wight Tourist, and Companion at Cowes*. Cowes, Isle of Wight: Robert Moir, 1830.

Vicinus, Martha, and Bea Nergaard, eds. *Ever Yours, Florence Nightingale: Selected Letters.* Cambridge, Mass.: Harvard University Press, 1990.

Victoria, Queen of Great Britain. *Leaves from the Journal of Our Life in the Highlands, from 1848 to 1861.* London: Smith, Elder and Co., 1868.

Vincent, John, ed. *Disraeli, Derby, and the Conservative Party.* Hassocks, Sussex, U.K.: Harvester, 1978.

Weintraub, Stanley. *Uncrowned King: The Life of Prince Albert.* New York: Free Press, 1997.

———. *Victoria: An Intimate Biography.* New York: Truman Talley, 1987.

Wells, H. G. *Experiment in Autobiography.* Vol. 1. London: Victor Gollancz, 1934.

Williams, Kate. *Becoming Queen Victoria.* New York: Ballantine Books, 2008.

Wilson, A. N. *Victoria: A Life.* New York: Penguin, 2014.

Woodham-Smith, Cecil. *Queen Victoria: Her Life and Times.* Vol. 1: *1819–1861.* London: Hamish Hamilton, 1972.

"A Working Man." "English Republicanism." *Fraser's Magazine.* June 1871, pp. 751–61.

Wright, Denis. *The Persians Among the English: Episodes in Anglo-Persian History.* London: I. B. Taurus and Co., 1985.

Wright, Patricia. *The Strange History of Buckingham Palace.* Stroud, Gloucestershire, U.K.: History Press, 2008.

Wyndham, Mrs. Hugh, ed. *Correspondence of Sarah Spencer, Lady Lyttelton, 1787–1870.* New York: Charles Scribner's Sons, 1912.

Zeepvat, Charlotte. *Prince Leopold: The Untold Story of Queen Victoria's Youngest Son.* Trupp, Stroud, Gloucestershire, U.K: Sutton, 1998.

Ziegler, Philip. *Melbourne: A Biography of William Lamb, 2nd Viscount Melbourne.* London: Collins, 1976.

Picture Credits

Art and Architecture Collection, Miriam and Ira D. Wallach Division of Art, Prints and Photographs,
    The New York Public Library, Astor, Lenox, and Tilden Foundations: 16, 18

Art & Picture Collection, The New York Public Library, Astor, Lenox, and Tilden Foundations: 168

Author's collection: 162, 165, 172, 194

© 2016 Malcolm Warrington / fotoLibra: 99

© Illustrated London News Ltd / Mary Evans: 4

General Research Division. The New York Public Library: 40

Library of Congress: 6, 78, 82, 91, 96, 97, 106, 108, 110, 181, 196, 197, 201, 202, 206

Mary Evans / Peter and Dawn Cope Collection: 68

Mary Evans Picture Library: 62, 104, 114, 115, 159

© National Portrait Gallery, London: 22, 38, 45, 52, 86

New York Public Library: 16, 18, 40, 168, 178, 184, 190

Print Collection, Mirian and Ira D. Wallach Division of Art, Prints and Photographs, The New York Public
    Library, Astor, Lenox and Tilden Foundations: 178, 184, 190

Royal Collection Trust / © Her Majesty Queen Elizabeth II 2016: x, 10, 15, 20, 24, 25, 26, 32, 35, 37, 42,
    46, 50, 61, 65, 70, 74, 75, 81, 83, 90, 92, 94, 102, 112, 124, 128, 133, 140, 142, 145, 152, 161, 164, 174,
    176, 185, 187, 188, 199, 204, 236

Used with permission of the James Smith Noel Collection at Louisiana State University in Shreveport: 2

Wellcome Library, London. Wellcome Images: 12, 13, 28, 31, 49, 54, 56, 58, 66, 67, 88, 117, 119, 120, 122,
    126, 130, 135, 138, 147, 148, 149, 170, 180, 182, 192, 214, 228

ADDITIONAL CAPTIONS

INDEX

NOTE: Page numbers in **bold** indicate images/pictures.

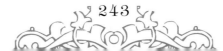